LET'S RECOVER YOU

YOUR JOURNALING GUIDE FOR EATING DISORDER RECOVERY

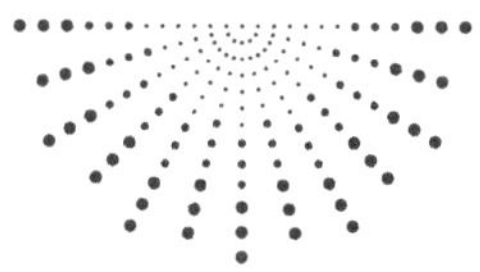

SOPHIE B

MAPLE LION PRESS

Published by Maple Lion Press
Unit 64956, PO Box 6945,
London, W1A 6US

Important Note: The content in this book and the accompanying resources provided by Recover You are not a substitute for professional medical advice. They are designed to complement and support those services provided by your primary care providers, not to replace them.

Content Warning: Throughout this guide the author will discuss eating disorders, associated dysphoria, body image, food, and appearance related issues. The author is committed to providing sensitive and responsible coverage of the abovementioned and wants you to be rest assured that they will not discuss measurements of any form or go into specific details of any associated harmful behaviours.

Print edition ISBN 978-1-8384372-4-4
E-book ISBN 978-1-8384372-5-1

Proofread by: Charlotte Lindsay Gray
Cover image created by: Benjamin Dawe

A CIP catalogue record for this title is available from the British Library.

To my loving husband,
I don't believe I would have met you,
had I not chosen recovery.

CONTENTS

About the book vii
A note from the author ix
Ten things... xi
My journaling journey xiii

1. Your journaling guide 1
2. Stage One 6
3. The Recover You Journaling Method 8
4. Space to Cope 11
5. Daily 15
6. Headspace 21
7. Routine 32
8. Reflections 41
9. Stage Two 61
10. Headspace 65
11. Routine 70
12. Reflections 72
13. Stage Three 96
14. Reflections 99
15. Moving forward 130

Journaling FAQs 133
Books I mentioned 139
Acknowledgments 141
About the Author 143

ABOUT THE BOOK

I wrote Let's Recover YOU with the determined adult in mind. You know who you are: you're the one who wants things to change, but doesn't know where to start, you're scared of what that change means and what that change might look like. Your heart desperately wants to recover, but your mind is filled with conflict and overwhelm. You might be waiting for treatment or already in therapy. You might have sought a diagnosis long ago or not even be diagnosed. Regardless of your circumstances, I believe this guide will serve you well.

Truthfully, I wanted to write this much earlier than I did, because I feel so passionately about the transformative process of journaling in recovery. However, something deep down in my core told me to wait. I had to be fully recovered first and continue to integrate all that I learned so I could process and share it with you today.

You can think of this guide like a friend holding your hand and showing you how to use journaling throughout the various stages of recovery you'll move through. I do want to fully acknowledge here that everybody's path will look different, and so as you move through the guide, please keep this in mind. I invite you to take what resonates and leave what doesn't.

Now, if you're wondering about the tone of this book, it's primarily based on my personal recovery experience from Orthorexia, Bulimia and Binge Eating Disorder. I share my personal anecdotes and journal entries throughout. You won't find me constantly referring to science and research papers, despite my background in those areas. And that's not to say there isn't value in that, I simply wanted to write this for you, from my heart to yours.

A NOTE FROM THE AUTHOR

Hi there! My name is Sophie and I'm really glad that you've found your way to me.

That said, I know you are here because you're probably doing it tough right now and I want to start by saying how proud I am of you for taking this step. For acknowledging that things need to change and for seeking out a way to help yourself.

Now trust me when I say I've been there. My life was once completely consumed by my eating disorder and truthfully, I couldn't ever imagine being free of it, nor in a strange way did I want to be. Sure, I wanted the disordered behaviours to stop, the physical side effects too, but I wasn't ready to let go of the identity I'd created around it. It was complicated. Eating disorders are complicated. But just because something is complicated it doesn't mean we can't overcome it.

I write this to you today, from a place better than I could ever have imagined. That person worried about a loss of identity is no more.

I'm finally living life on my terms, fully recovered and grateful for each day.

I'm telling you this because I want you to know that recovery is possible. It may seem far from reach right now. It may seem really daunting too, but you're here because there's a big part of you that wants to change and right now, that's what counts.

It's okay if there are parts of you that are scared and unsure if you can. It's okay if there are parts of you that doubts journaling and how it can even help you. But the main thing right now is that you're here and willing to give it a chance.

I've created this guide for you based on my own path of recovery, in which I used my journal to cope, understand and heal from my eating disorder. Throughout these pages I'm going to guide you through exactly how I did it, and share my method, insights, and tips to get you started.

With love,

Sophie B

TEN THINGS…

I WISH SOMEONE HAD TOLD ME WHEN I STARTED OUT IN RECOVERY.

1. You're going to cry a lot and that's okay. Crying really helps heal.

2. There are going to be days when you think you can't do it, like it's not possible and maybe no one ever truly recovers, but they do, and something tells me that you will be one of them.

3. You're not broken. If this thought crops up for you, know that it once did for me too *(a lot)*. I would worry, that I couldn't be 'fixed' or that I was destined to live my life with this disorder, turns out neither were true. When you ask for help, share what's going on with you and commit to making changes, you *can* recover.

4. You're not alone. When I first heard someone else in recovery say how terrified they had become of the supermarket I could have cried *(I probably did later that day)*. I truly thought I was the only one experiencing that. So please know you're not alone in your struggles even if your brain tries to tell you otherwise.

5. There will be days where you feel like you're making progress and then you wake up the next, feeling like you're back to square one. But trust me, you never are. Roll with the ups and downs but keep moving forward.

6. It's going to take a while. All good things do, right? For me this was probably one of the hardest things to come to terms with, I just wanted my ED to be gone and quick smart! But recovery takes repeated action over time. Be kind and patient with yourself *(Don't worry, I've got tips to help)*.

7. Your body is going to go through physical changes and whilst that can be hard to navigate and accept initially, you will get through it and come out the other side appreciating all your body does for you.

8. Learn to be your own biggest cheerleader! Yup. It's time to cheer for YOU! Tell yourself you are proud of you every day! Celebrate your recovery wins! Hype yourself up. It might sound cheesy, but it's important to foster a kind, supportive relationship with the person you spend the most time with… you!

9. Hold onto hope. Always. There is always hope and it's a powerful emotion.

10. Lean on others when you need to. Don't try and tough this out alone. Speak up when you're struggling. Talk to those you trust about what you're going through or find yourself an in-person or online support group. It makes a world of difference to your recovery when you talk about your troubles.

MY JOURNALING JOURNEY

I was a stressed-out, thirty something, full-time university student battling an eating disorder that I didn't want to admit to. Overtime, my Orthorexia had become Bulimia which then eventually developed into Binge Eating Disorder. I had just gotten out of a long-term relationship, and I lived in a different country to any of my family, so my support network was limited as were my funds for any sort of private treatment.

I'd sought out the help of a medical professional and been told the wait for any public assistance would be a six-month minimum and even then, it would be unlikely as my case was not deemed severe enough to be a priority. In the meantime, I was to start on some medication to help with my mood and that was that.

I realised then that if I wanted to get started with my recovery asap, I'd have to find a way to help myself and as daunting as it seemed, I wasn't about to let this illness take everything from me. I began my search for alternative *(read free)* methods of help.

My first port of call was social media which was tricky given that a lot of what was online had led me down a dark path in the first place. I followed a bunch of self-love and 'food freedom' accounts in an attempt to garner some sort of encouragement or advice, but their content didn't really resonate with me. I couldn't go from having a full-on eating disorder, paired with viciously negative body image and a brutal inner critic to loving everything about myself and eating freely. It was too big of a leap to make. So, I scrapped that idea.

Next, I tried a bunch of free online resources but most focused on building coping skills and I couldn't quite get my head around that. I wasn't in the headspace yet to realise that I used my eating disorder to cope. Then, one day during my search a lightbulb flickered on in my head. I recalled a lecture I'd attended where someone had spoken of recovering from Anorexia using journaling. I don't know why I hadn't thought of it sooner. Though if I'm truthful, I'd sort of dismissed the power of journaling. I remember at the time thinking, so you just write out your feelings and then you're magically better? Yeah right! So, if that's you right now, I get it, but please hear me out…

Once I was stocked with notebooks, I started writing. My practice was a little haphazard, I just wrote whatever came to mind, but it felt really nice to put down on the pages everything that was going on in my head. It almost felt like I'd talked to someone about it. So, I started to use my journal whenever I felt I needed it. Every time I started to panic; I wrote it out. Every time I felt angry or confused, you guessed it, I wrote it out. It wasn't a quick fix nor was my path linear, it took time, patience and a lot of back and forth, but eventually it helped me to break the cycle of physically damaging behaviours. Then as I continued, it helped me piece together what had led me down this path in the first place.

Now, I want to reiterate, I'm not suggesting this guide as an alternative to seeking out the help of medical professionals. However, the reality of the situation is that regardless of what treatment path you venture down, there is still a lot of space in between appointments. Having a self-directed, self-supportive practice such as journaling can be an absolute treasure and help you through those times. I figure if it worked for me, it could very well work for you. I was someone who didn't have much faith in the concept when I started out but now, I can only sing its praises. I wouldn't be where I am today without it and I'm that passionate about its benefits that I've made it my mission to spread the word.

1

YOUR JOURNALING GUIDE

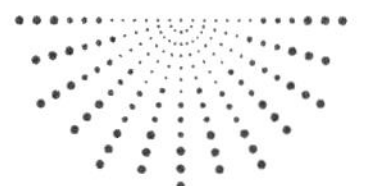

What is journaling & why should I journal in recovery?

Put simply, journaling is a way of recording your personal thoughts, feelings and life events on paper. It's a tool for self-reflection and making sense of the world around you. The act of writing about these topics and the process of putting pen to paper is in itself therapeutic. When living with an eating disorder, often it can be hard to verbalise what we are going through. Journaling provides an outlet whereby we can freely express ourselves without fear of judgement. It can help us to organise our thoughts, gain clarity on things that keep milling about in our head and to release pent up emotions we didn't even know were there too.

Why follow this guide?

Looking back, I can see that if I had some sort of structure and guidance in my journaling practice, it would have accelerated my progress or at least given it more direction. As it was, I just wrote sporadically about this and that, which was certainly a huge help, but it did feel a little directionless. Plus, over the years I've found consistency is key with journaling and if you're spending your energy wondering what to write about or how to get started, it slows up the whole process and it can even put you off making it a go-to in your routine. And whilst there are many different prompt packs and workbooks out there, I think it's important to have something tailored to eating disorder recovery, especially from someone who used it successfully in their own.

What the guide covers...

How to establish new routines and positive habits to support your recovery. It invites you to explore your relationship with yourself and others, body image, confidence, self-worth, food feelings, health, movement and much much more. Plus, it takes you through how to use your journal as a space to cope and self-manage your emotions, whenever you need it.

What the guide doesn't cover...

The nutritional aspect of eating disorders such as specific advice on how to return to 'normal' eating patterns. However, I do invite you to think about your food and eating plan in stage one and to then explore your relationship with food in stage two. I realise that might sound scary right now, but we build up to it over time. And remember, you only need to tackle that when you're ready. You're in charge here.

How is the guide structured?

I've designed this guide for you based on my own path of recovery. It's divided up into three consecutive stages to be undertaken at your own pace. This is because the things you'll need to address in the early days of recovery will differ greatly from those several months in. As your recovery progresses, so does each stage. You'll start with small, accessible tasks and only tackle more in-depth topics once you're feeling ready.

I suggest everyone starts at stage one, no matter where you're at in your recovery because it does set you up for the other stages. However, if you have been in recovery for some time, feel free to move through it a bit quicker and only address what you feel is needed. For everyone else, I want you to take it slow and steady.

Ps – If you run into any challenges when putting pen to paper, be sure to check out the Journaling FAQs at the back of the book.

The diagram that follows outlines the three consecutive Recover You Stages and our associated thought process.

The top row shows the path our mind takes when we have a negative thought, and the bottom row shows the different stages of the course.

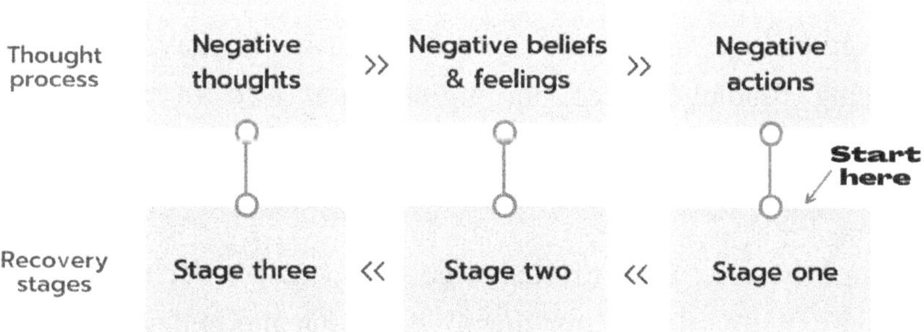

Now the first thing you'll probably notice is that the course stages flow in a backwards direction and that's because we're actually going to work backwards.

Now if you're wondering, but why work backwards?

Well, that's because breaking the chain of negative actions is our priority since those things are directly impacting our physical health. Those are the things which pose the greatest immediate risk to us and can cause long term damage to our bodies; hence we need to tackle them first.

Once those aspects are under control, you can start to physically heal. You'll find your mood improves, chances are you'll sleep better too and that then creates a solid base to start tackling the mental aspects of stages two and three.

Plus, if you're anything like me, you've probably buried a lot of feelings for a very long time, so tackling them outright without having any new coping strategies in place *(like the ones we're going to introduce in stage one)* might well trigger some of those old negative behaviours that we use to cope. And we don't want that.

Let's break down each stage a little further…

In stage one we target our negative actions and behaviours such as bingeing, food avoidance, purging etc, then once we have our new supportive systems in place and start to break the cycle of physical behaviours, we move on to stage two.

In stage two we start to challenge our negative feelings and the beliefs which underpin our negative actions and behaviours, using our journal.

Then in stage three, we go one step further and start to question why we are having those negative thoughts in the first place. We then aim to break the pattern between our negative thoughts automatically triggering our negative feelings.

I realise it might sound like a lot right now, but fear not, I'll be guiding you through every step of the way.

What do I need to get started?

An A4 notepad - Any A4 notepad with lines will do. My personal preference is always a Pukka Pad which they sell on Amazon, but any other notepad works too.

Pen *(s)* - of your choosing! *(I'm a biro kinda girl)*

A pad of sticky notes *(post-it's, whatever you call them)*, we're going to use these as bookmarks *(you'll only need five total, so just one pack will do)*

And ideally a comfortable space where you won't be disturbed.

A quick note before we get into it…

As you work your way through the prompts and activities, it might bring up some things that you want to chat over with the healthcare professionals in your life. If it does, please don't hesitate to reach out to them, that's what they are there for. And if ever you have any questions for me, please feel free to get in touch and I'll do my best to answer them or at least point you to someone who can. My details can be found at the back of this book or on the Recover You website.

Now take a deep breath in for four through your nose, pause for four at the top and then release out through your mouth for four.

(This is a 'box' breathing technique that you can practice anytime and ideally before you sit down to journal)

Ready to get into it? Let's go…

2
STAGE ONE

BREAKING HABITS

"You can't change what happened, but you can choose what happens next." - Mel Robbins.

Your goal: To reduce harmful behaviours and negative actions towards yourself.

Okay, so this stage is all about reducing any harmful physical behaviours you might be engaging in. I won't list them all here, but it includes things such as bingeing, avoiding eating, purging. You get the idea. In this stage you don't have to question or delve into why you do these things, the focus here is to just break the physical cycle. The stages after are where we start to dig deeper into the whys behind the behaviour. But for now, it's important to just focus on one thing at a time.

How you're going to get there...

You're going to learn how to use your journal to interject and cope when those harmful behaviours rear their head. Plus, you're going to revamp your routine, reflect on a few topics and build a system of new positive habits to create a supportive environment for your recovery and set you up for success.

Now if you're thinking, sure… easier said than done. You're also going to figure out what your motivation to recover is. That's going to be your driver in all of this, but more on that later.

What is the suggested timeframe?

The journaling guide is designed to be completed at your own pace. Whilst there are commonalities in all of our experiences, everyone's recovery is going to look different, so take as much time as you need, where you need it. You can think of this book as a companion on your recovery journey instead of something to rush through and complete. I want it to feel like a friend helping to guide you through.

That said, I do suggest staying in stage one until you start to break the cycle of some of your physically harmful behaviours. I have a table at the end of each stage which details how to tell when you're ready to move on to the next stage. I personally remained in stage one for several months, so don't feel you need to rush. Recovery takes time, new habits take time to form and stay with us. So do exactly that, take your time and be proud that you've committed to taking steps in the right direction.

Now, let's move onto setup…

3

THE RECOVER YOU JOURNALING METHOD

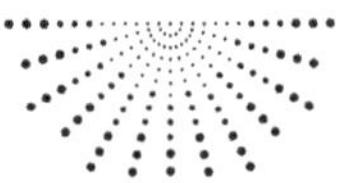

IMPORTANT, DON'T SKIP THIS ONE

I designed the Recover You Journaling Method (RYJM) so you can get the full benefit and support from your journaling practice in your recovery.

Whilst more 'traditional' journaling *(where you follow a prompt or write freely)* is amazingly beneficial on its own, I found that using a multi-pronged approach to journaling in recovery works best.

So, with that in mind…

I created five different journal sections to each serve their own unique purpose: *Space to Cope, Daily, Routine, Headspace and Reflections.*

I'll be breaking down each section in more detail shortly, but for now, take a look at the following table and then we'll get your journal set up with the RYJM.

Section	What is it?	What's its purpose?	When to use it
Space to Cope	A section of allocated blank pages where you can write freely.	To let out whatever's going on. Sometimes that emotion can be hard to verbalise so putting it down on paper can help.	When feeling overwhelmed and compelled to engage in a harmful physical ED behaviour.
Daily	Five questions to be completed each day.	To form the habit of getting in touch with emotions on the daily and help improve mindset.	Daily & preferably in the morning as it helps set the tone for the day.
Routine	A series of tasks to revamp your routine.	To create a mentally and physically supportive environment for your recovery.	At the beginning of each stage, I suggest reviewing it.
Headspace	A section to explore where you're at & why you want to recover via guided journal prompts.	To get clear on what you're working towards and why you want to get there.	It's always best to start out slow so I often recommend one prompt every few days or one weekly.
Reflections	A series of more in-depth journal prompts that cover a vast range of topics.	To increase understanding of the self and address topics which may impact your ED & your recovery from it.	As with Headspace, start out slow. Address one prompt every few days or one prompt weekly.

How to set up your journal

Have you got your A4 notepad, pen and pad of sticky notes? *(If not, see the previous section: Your journaling guide, for more details.)* If so, let's set up our journals!

If you're more of a visual learner, I've created a video on how to do this too, just head on over to the Recover You website and you'll find it there.

Start with the heading: Headspace at the very front of your notebook. You can write it at the top of the first page or mark it with a sticky note *(sort of like a bookmark sticking out the top of the page, but you don't have to with this one since it's located at the front of the book.)*

Allow yourself about fifteen pages for the Headspace section, then after it, put the heading Routine, you can mark it with a sticky note. Allow roughly ten pages for the Routine section, you might not need all of them but it's better to have extra.

After the tenth page of Routine, it's time to put the Reflections heading. This is where you'll do most of your writing so be sure to leave plenty of space.

Next, about halfway through your notebook, mark the page with Daily and add in a sticky note or bookmark of your choosing. This is the section you'll be visiting each day so make sure it's clear where to find it.

Finally, about three quarters into your notebook, closer to the back, mark the page with Space to Cope and of course, add in your sticky note, fold the corner of the page over or use a fancy divider.

Once you've set up your notebook with the appropriate sections, you're ready to get started.

Ps – this is just how I set up my notebook, if you want to give something else a whirl, go for it. It's about making this work for you.

4

SPACE TO COPE

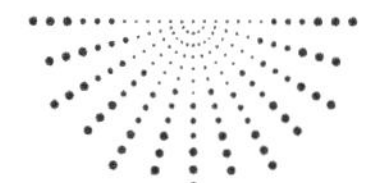

I want to take you through this section first because it is going to play a significant role in breaking the cycle of harmful physical behaviours.

The idea with *Space to Cope* is that you use it whenever you feel compelled to engage in a harmful behaviour.

I'll explain how…

Right before you engage in a binge, purge or other harmful ed behaviour there's typically a moment where you feel emotion and thoughts that you can't express. It might be panic or overwhelm, it could be anger or sadness. Whatever it is, your thoughts typically start spiralling and get very loud. The emotions feel overwhelming, and you find yourself searching for your most 'reliable' solution, an ed behaviour.

So, the new goal here is to learn to interrupt this pattern and to use your journal to do so.

Here's how...

The next time you feel those emotions welling up, whatever they might be, I want you to grab your pen and journal, turn to your *Space to Cope* and write out whatever's going on. It can be complete gibberish, just random words on a page, but what it helps you to do is break the automatic cycle of negative feelings triggering negative behaviours.

I used to call it my 'panic pages', which I know isn't the most soothing of names but that's essentially what it was for me. Every time I felt panic well up and the urge to binge or purge arise, I would tell myself to pause and go to the pages.

I would ask myself: *what's going on? why am I feeling like this? (You could even write this at the top of your Space to Cope section.)*

I would tell myself that if I still wanted to carry out whatever behaviour it was I could, but I had to give myself five minutes.

As I would start to write, typically the panic would pass. I'd often cry and sort of soothe myself via my journal and after the five minutes was up, my urge to engage in any harmful behaviours had typically passed too.

It might seem a little strange at first, or it might even be hard to intervene with yourself, but I invite you to give it your best shot.

Plus, if you do use it on the regular, it can provide you with some great insight into your behaviours and help identify any patterns which might occur too. If you're working with a mental health professional, it can be beneficial to take along your entries to a session. Sometimes in the moment it can be hard to remember how you've been feeling and something might keep on cropping up in your journal which they can help you with.

. . .

An important note:

Whilst it's important to write what's on your mind, I don't want these pages or your journaling practice to be a space where you berate yourself or reinforce negative beliefs. I'll explain what I mean by that a little more…

When living with an ed, it's very common for it to take over our inner voice and dialogue. It typically says very mean things and it can be hard to separate yourself from them.

Now, a key part of recovery is learning to differentiate between your own voice and that of your eating disorder and that takes practice over time, but we'll talk more on this later.

For now, I just want you to focus on one key thing: *I feel.*

If you find yourself in your *Space to Cope* writing mean things about yourself, or you know you have a tendency or temptation to express that negative inner dialogue on the pages, I want you to take a moment to recognise that and re-write it with 'I feel'.

For example:

Your ed voice or mean inner dialogue might be raging and you're replaying the thought 'I am stupid' or 'I am useless' over and over (things which you never are ♡). You might be tempted in the moment to write this, but instead I want you to try and catch yourself and write 'I feel' instead of 'I am'.

It may seem small but it's a very important distinction to make. It creates separation from the words as your identity.

Whilst you might feel stupid, you are not stupid. It's just a feeling and feelings come and go. They are temporary. But the more you tell yourself and label yourself with them negatively, the more you will believe them to be true even when they're not.

It's a simple but effective way of changing your inner dialogue and whilst it takes practice to catch it, it will start to become a habit overtime.

5
DAILY

The next section I want to run you through before we get to the more 'traditional' journaling, is one to be completed on (you guessed it) the daily!

This section is a daily check in with yourself via your journal comprising of five questions. Ideally, it's to be completed each morning as it can help set the tone for the day. However, if that's not possible for you, anytime of day is fine, you'll still get the same benefit. It's always important to remember that everyone's recovery and day looks different, there is no right and wrong here.

Each day, I want you to ask yourself…

How am I feeling today?

Then jot it down in your journal.

E.g., I feel sad, but better than yesterday.

Use this as a chance to make that distinction again – I feel, instead of I am.

E.g., Today, I feel sad as opposed to, I am sad.

Now, if you feel like you have no idea how to answer this question, I want you to know that is completely understandable. So often with eating disorders we detach from our feelings. We push them away for whatever reason that might be, and we simply don't allow ourselves to feel. So, when asked it can often feel overwhelming or you might not even know *what* you feel. My suggestion here is to instead try and describe the feeling using a colour.

Ask yourself: Is there a colour that represents how I'm feeling in my mind and body today?

Then jot that down in your journal instead.

Next up, I want you to ask…

What was one challenge yesterday?

E.g. - fighting the urge to obsessively check my body and scroll through social media.

It might seem counterintuitive to focus on the negative, but I'm a big believer in taking lessons from our struggles, they teach us something about what we can do differently.

Once you have written down the thing you found most challenging yesterday. I want you to ask yourself: *Can I reframe that today? Can I adjust my reaction? Or can I adjust the situation?*

For example: If you struggled with bodychecking yesterday. Could you reframe that as: I did struggle with bodychecking yesterday, but I made it through and today is a new day. Or could you adjust the situation, and say today, I'm going to make a note of how many times I bodycheck and then reduce it by one tomorrow.

Now I realise it sounds easier said than done and, in some situations, it simply isn't possible to change or reframe it. But the aim of this question is about learning to pause and reflect on some of the things we're doing that might not be so helpful for us and moving forward, how we can improve them.

Let's move on, next up…

What was one positive yesterday?

E.g. - binge free day, not guilting myself, getting out of bed, taking time to journal.

You can write anything here, any positive no matter how seemingly small you might think it is, whatever it is, write it down.

If you're mind jumps to the negative here or you feel like you don't deem anything as a positive, instead ask yourself: *What did I learn? What's a vote for my recovery?*

E.g. – I learnt that I am resilient because I got through yesterday and I'll get through today too. Showing up on the pages and writing in my journal is a vote for my recovery.

Celebrating your everyday wins and positive actions in recovery can really help to keep your motivation flowing, plus, on those days where you doubt just how far you've come (we all have them) you can come back, flick through the pages and see it all there before you.

Moving on to the next question…

What's something nice I can do for myself today?

Even if you don't feel like it, you must learn to show yourself kindness in this time and I find writing it out as a commitment in your journal makes a habit of doing so. You're going through one heck of a lot so having something nice to look forward to can really help make the day feel a little brighter. It doesn't have to be anything grand, something simple such as planning to watch an episode of a comedy show that night (because laughing even when you don't feel like it really helps) or reading a favourite book before bed does the trick too. This is your time to show yourself the same kindness that you show to others.

Next up…

What are three things I am grateful for today?

This can be absolutely anything. From the chance to recover through to the roof over your head. The idea here is to focus on the good in our life and be grateful for what we do have even when our disorder might be making us feel miserable.

Practicing gratitude is not to deny the existence of our problems or pretend that everything is okay, instead it's to help us see the things we do have and be thankful for them, despite what we might be going through.

And truthfully, there will be some days where it doesn't matter how grateful you try to be, you just don't feel it. And that's okay. Recovery is tough, so go easy on yourself. The main thing here is forming the habit and making it part of your daily routine.

And finally…

Write out an affirmation for the day.

If you're new to the world of affirmations, the idea here is to have a phrase which you can repeat in your head or even out loud to yourself throughout the day. The goal is to use it to help you challenge and overcome negative thoughts. It can be anything motivating that resonates with you, just bear in mind it doesn't always have to be positive it can be neutral too. The main thing is that it's somewhat believable to you.

Here are some of my favourites to get you started:

I am strong, smart and capable
Today, I take action in spite of fear
I am strong and resilient
I am reclaiming my life
I am supported and loved
I allow myself to move forward in life
I am worthy of love and respect
I am worthy of recovery, I value myself
Today, I choose me
I am proud of my progress

If you're reading these and finding they don't resonate, you can try more neutral versions too.

For example:

I am finding recovery hard, but I am trying

Every day is a challenge, but I am strong

The key with affirmations is that they have to work for you. There is no point in repeating something that doesn't resonate or feels out of alignment with where you're at. Play around with what works best for you.

Handy hint: set some affirmations as timed phone reminders throughout the day, to boost your mood when you need it most.

The five daily questions again in sum:

How am I feeling today?

What was one challenge yesterday?

What was one positive yesterday?

What's something nice I can do for myself today?

What are three things I am grateful for today?

And then top it off with an affirmation.

Ps - I know completing the same tasks each day might seem a bit monotonous, but it's the only way we form awesome new habits. Plus, this practice is a bit of time out just for you, and you need that right now.

It's finally time to get into some journaling, let's move into *Headspace.*

6

HEADSPACE

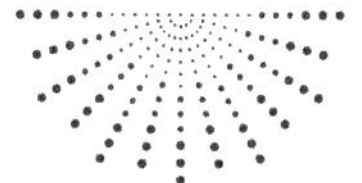

Turn to the Headspace section of your journal. It's time to get into your first prompt.

Prompt: Find your WHY. This is going to serve as your motivator throughout your recovery. When times get tough, I want you to refer back to your why.

Ask yourself. Why do you want to recover?

Think about...

What is motivating you to be here working through this book?

Is there someone *(other than yourself)* that you want to recover for?

(I just want to mention here, I do believe part of wanting to recover must be for you, however I do think another person can inspire you to recover and form part of your motivation)

How is life going for you right now? How could your recovery change that for the better?

Write down whatever comes to mind.

For example:

I want to recover because I am sick of living my life this way. My mind is never free.

I want to recover because I want to go after my dream job, and I won't be able to if I keep putting all my time and energy elsewhere.

I want to recover for my kids.

Write as much or as little as you like.

Now, if nothing springs to mind straight away, don't worry. Instead reframe the question and think about…

What aspects of your disorder do you dislike?

I guarantee there are some, otherwise you wouldn't be here.

For me, I loathed the control it had over me and how it preoccupied my mind at all times. It was utterly exhausting. The enjoyment it sucked out of social occasions was another thing.

Once you've written those out. I want you to turn your reasons into a positive statement for you to refer back to.

For example: If you wrote, I loathe the control it has over me. This becomes, I want to regain control over my life.

It's more empowering this way.

My why was: I want to be present in my relationships and enjoy my life.

I realise that might seem really broad, or maybe even obvious, but at the time, I did neither of those things and for me, using this as my *why* worked.

Each time I started to spiral or doubt my recovery, I used this to remind myself of the possibilities a recovered life could bring.

I found it really helped to tap into all the feelings that went along with that. How being present and connected would feel. How allowing myself to enjoy something would feel. It gave me hope.

Your WHY can be broad *(like mine)* or more specific, but the most important thing is that it resonates with you. When you read it back to yourself it should fill you with a sense of determination.

Handy hint: make your WHY easily accessible so it's always there when you need it. You could put a note in your phone, make it your screen background, pin it to your desktop, pin it to your bathroom mirror or even set it as a daily phone reminder.

Prompt: For those of you that have experienced relapse or feel 'stuck' in your recovery, I want you to ask yourself: *What am I doing differently this time? What will I do differently moving forward?*

For example:

Recovery is different this time because I have learnt from the past and set myself up with a more supportive environment.

Recovery is different this time because I'm here giving a new journaling method a try, I have a better support network and I'm attending weekly peer support groups.

I'm choosing to move forward in my recovery by committing to daily journaling and weekly therapy sessions.

Prompt: Do you have hesitations or fears about recovery? What's the first thing you think of when I ask that question?

If you struggle to articulate what exactly it is, write down the feelings that come up instead.

I want you to be brutally honest here. Whatever comes to mind, write it down. Don't worry about trying to form your thoughts, just let things flow out of you without judgement.

Come back here once you're done and we'll talk a little more.

* * *

You're back! I am so proud of you for getting that out.

Now take a deep breath in, pause for four and release.

Better? I hope so.

Whatever you just wrote down, whatever you're feeling throughout your body, I want you to know that all of your feelings here are completely valid. It's only natural to feel fearful or have reservations about change.

You see, as humans we often find change scary because we can't anticipate the exact outcome. Our brains don't really like that, they'd much prefer a predictable outcome, even if it is a negative one. So, when we're faced with recovery and a lot of new changes, it's only natural that hesitations crop up because our brain doesn't know what to expect. Fortunately, we do have the power to hit the override switch and re-train our brain. Yay!

Here's how…

We're going to tell it some new stories…

Our fear of change is based on stories we tell ourselves or things that have happened to us in the past. We tend to re-hash these moments in our minds and avoid making any changes because our brain thinks that this is best, it's trying to keep us 'safe'.

So, what we can do here is give it new stories to soak up where change is powerful and associated with positive outcomes.

Let's give that a go...

Prompt: I want you to write down some of the positive thing's recovery can bring to your life.

For example:

Recovery will mean I am more present with the people I love.

Recovery will give me more energy.

Recovery will make me feel more emotionally stable.

If it feels too difficult to imagine, instead ask yourself:

What would you love to do more of in life?

What makes you smile?

What brings you joy?

What brings energy in?

It could be a person, place, or activity. I want you to write down absolutely anything that lights up your world.

I want to share my personal ones that I wrote during my own recovery:

I would love to be able to cook again.

I would love to be able to go out for dinner with a free mind.

I would love to go on dates.

Prompt: Now, I want you to take all of the positives you've thought of and link them up with your recovery. These are your new stories.

For example: Recovery means I will be able to cook again. Recovery means I will go out for dinners without worry. Recovery means I will go on dates (I did, and I met my now husband!)

Whenever you feel fear creeping in or those hesitations of whether or not you can actually recover, I want you to come back to this space and tell yourself these stories. Remember they're here anytime you need them.

Handy hint: An empowering affirmation here can be, I choose recovery. When old fears try to push through, repeat this phrase to yourself.

Prompt: What does recovery mean to you? What does it mean to be recovered? What is your definition of recovery? What is your goal?

You might want to read this before you put pen to paper…

This one might have you stumped. You might be thinking, I just want to be recovered, isn't that enough? But what I'm asking you to think about here is, what does that involve? Recovery and being recovered means different things for different people.

For a long time, I didn't define what recovery would look like for me. Sure, I'd committed to it, but I hadn't ever imagined what it would fully encompass. About two and a half years into my recovery I started to wonder if I was fully recovered. I'd stopped with the physically damaging behaviours and that had been my goal, but I still didn't feel great about myself. I didn't feel comfortable calling myself recovered because something felt off.

When I dissected the components of what being recovered meant to me. I realised that there was still work to be done with my body image and inner critic.

That's the thing, recovery isn't just about the physical, it's about so much more.

This is why I want you to think about what recovery means to you and get clear on your own definition or goals. Having clarity on what you're working towards can really help you get there.

Now I realise it might be a big ask to think of such a thing at this time, but I think it will be really beneficial for you in the long run.

I've included my own definition below, for you to think on.

To be recovered means that I no longer engage or consider engaging in harmful eating disorder related behaviours nor do I use said behaviours to cope with my problems.

My relationship with both food and movement is positive and does not dominate my life. My self-worth is built on my values and experiences, not my body. I value myself as I am today and understand that whilst negative body image thoughts can still occur for me, I do not act upon them and typically have a realistic view of my body.

Full recovery encompasses all of this for me and allows me to joyfully live my life, without fear of relapse.

How does that sit with you? Are they goals you see yourself working towards? Or are there things you'd add in or leave out?

I'm going to give you two options here:

One, you might want to try and write out your own definition. I realise that it can be hard to know what exactly you want at this point, but you might, if so, it's time to put pen to paper.

Or if that feels a bit much, option two is to write out five recovery goals for yourself.

I'd aim for two physical goals, two mental goals and one lifestyle goal.

What I mean by that is:

Physical goals: stop restricting, stop overexercising.

Mental goals: repair relationship with food, feel better about self.

Lifestyle goal: get adequate rest each day.

We all have different challenges to overcome, so think of your own most pressing issues and write them down.

Once you have your five goals, you can take it one step further and plan an action for each to be completed this week.

For example:

If one of your physical goals was to stop restricting, your action could be to commit to eating breakfast each day or adding in a snack.

If one of your lifestyle goals was to get adequate rest each day, your action could be to commit to being in bed by 9pm each night or letting yourself put your feet up on a night.

Now I realise this additional 'action' step can be really challenging to come up with and it might not be something you're able to do on your own. If you feel so inclined, this is one you could discuss with someone in your life that you trust, a healthcare professional or even a recovery coach.

Because goals are great, but we need action to recover.

Prompt: Write a breakup letter to your eating disorder.

Hear me out on this one. I know it can be tempting to skip this prompt. It might feel too much, or you might think it seems ridiculous. But I invite you to think of this prompt the way I do…

I like to think of it as similar to a breakup, and a bad one at that. You've got to a point where you're sick of their shit. You're done living your life like this. You want change, but you're scared. You way up the pros and cons. *Maybe the familiar is better?* But you're so unhappy. *Maybe it will get better?* But it hasn't so far…

You get the idea.

Writing this letter isn't saying goodbye for ever, instead, think of it as a way of outlining all your intentions, why you're done with it and why you deserve better.

It doesn't mean it's done, but you are taking a stance. *(They might try and re-kindle things six months later when they drop some of your stuff off, but you're not interested anymore, you've moved on.)*

And if I still haven't sold you on it, feel free to move onto the next prompt.

Prompt: Write a journal entry as your future self.

I'll explain what I mean by that a bit more…

This goes back to the idea of creating some new positive recovery-based stories for our brain to soak up. It's an opportunity to try your hand at some future journaling, a technique where you write your journals as *(you guessed it)* your future self. It's a chance to explore what the recovered version of your life will look like and a space to dream of the possibilities that lie ahead. This is also a great exercise to do when you've had a heavy journaling session or a difficult day.

With this technique you're going to write your journal entry as your future-self but as if you are living in the present moment.

Here's what I mean by that:

I wake filled with gratitude for the life I have. I scored that job I really wanted, and I work with lovely, kind people. Plus, I get Friday's off, how good is that! It's a crisp, sunny day outside. The leaves have just started to fall. I feel peace in my soul for the first time in a long time. I'm so proud of how far I've come. I've just booked a trip to New York; I've always wanted to go there. It feels like a dream.

I realise it might feel a bit strange or silly to write this type of entry, but the idea is that you're changing your beliefs about yourself. You're bringing in new positive stories, even if they aren't true *(yet)*.

Now it's your turn…

I want you to imagine being recovered. Take a moment to close your eyes and imagine all the glittering possibilities that lie ahead. Take some deep breaths in and out here too.

Ask yourself: How does life look? How do you feel? What fantastic things are you doing?

Dream big here. Get as carried away as you like. You could write about a place you'll travel to or even a 'day in the life'.

Whatever it is, take a moment *(or several)* to share it in your journal.

Handy hint: This is the perfect exercise to do when you've had a heavy journaling session or a difficult day. It's a great way to zoom out and see that so many brighter days lay ahead.

A word on positive thinking.

I know I encourage you to think of the positive in situations a lot, but I want to be clear here, I am not suggesting that you force yourself to be positive at all times. Sure, we want to cultivate a more positive mindset to help us cope, but we don't want to do it at the expense of our other emotions.

It's important to acknowledge, sit with and experience a whole spectrum of feelings and emotions. That's part of what makes us human. Plus, working through all that tough stuff is what sets us up for long term success.

When I encourage you to put a positive spin on things, it's so that you can try and use it as motivation to keep going in your recovery. It's so that you can learn to talk yourself around and reframe situations so that you can grow through them. And last but certainly not least, it's so you can learn to be kinder and more loving towards yourself.

With that in mind, let's move onto re-writing routines....

7

ROUTINE

Our routine can play a huge role in forming our mindset each day. I'm sure you've had one of those days; you wake up late, you rush out the house, then everything you encounter that day feels like a pain and you end up carrying that feeling with you all day. Rushed, frustrated, and honestly, a bit defeated. Now, not only does our routine impact our mindset but it has the power to support or disrupt our physical behaviours too. And in the case of eating disorders, that is so incredibly important.

Taking the time to recognise when and where your harmful physical behaviours are occurring, will give you the opportunity to challenge them. Re-writing your routine is a chance to create a mentally and physically supportive environment for your recovery.

The aim of your new routine is to use it to stop or significantly reduce whatever harmful physical behaviours you are engaging in *(meal skipping, bingeing, bodychecking etc)*.

The examples I have included throughout the routine section are based on my old routines and the changes I made to break free of my damaging behaviours. I cannot emphasise enough the importance of creating a supportive routine for yourself. It's truly life changing. I realise it seems like a big task with a lot of changes, but I assure you, it will make the world of difference.

Task: Think about your average weekday. What time of day do you struggle with disordered behaviours the most? What time of day do you struggle with disordered thoughts the most?

The idea here is to identify your most problematic areas and then in task two you'll plan for them moving forward.

For example:

In a morning I tend to leave the house without eating. I also have a hard time getting dressed without body checking. Once on public transport I start to constantly compare myself to others. Once at work or university, I'm quite busy so I don't really have too much time to think about things but once I get home, I find it difficult. Night times are the hardest, this is the time where I tend to binge and over exercise. I really don't know how to overcome this, but I know I want to. My harmful behaviours need to stop.

From this, we can see that mornings and night times are the most challenging.

I want you to repeat this exercise for the weekend too. I know this can be tricky as it is often more unpredictable but give it a go.

Ps - If you're someone whose routine constantly changes and it's near impossible to break down a typical day, instead just try and find one hour of the day where you can create consistency and where you typically struggle. That might be an hour in the morning before you leave the house, or it could be an hour in an evening before bed. The idea here is still the same, to identify your most problematic areas.

Once you have that information, it's time to re-write your routine…

Task: Step 1: Break down the problematic areas of your routine *(even if it's the whole day)*, just write it out best you can. In addition, write down any associated feelings that you recall which come up during this time too.

For example:

Current morning routine:

6.30am Wake up, check messages, emails (feel stressed) scroll through social media (engage in comparison).

6.45am Get up, search for something to wear and bodycheck, start to trash talk myself.

7.00am Slap on some sunscreen, feel upset, defeated already.

7.15am Leave house with no breakfast.

Task: Step 2: It's time to create your new supportive routine! The goal here is to give yourself a blueprint to follow that will serve you better.

New morning routine:

6.30am Wake up, grab journal and write some waking thoughts.

6.45am Get up, grab my comfy clothes which I laid out the night before, no body checking allowed, just get those clothes on.

7.00am Wash face, moisturise, sunscreen, keep my focus laser sharp, complete one step after another.

7.15am Breakfast, pre-planned (non-negotiable).

The idea is that you don't give yourself time to dwell. The steps are clear and once one is complete, it's onto the next.

For those of you that prefer a more visual representation, I've created the table below to help break it down.

Time of day	Current routine	Associated feelings	Current ED behaviour	New coping method or behaviour
Morning	Wake-up, check phone & social media	Feel stressed, engage in comparison	Start to berate myself	Grab journal upon waking instead of phone and jot down some first thoughts of the day
Morning	Get dressed & ready for the day	Negative self-talk	Bodycheck	Lay out comfy clothes the night before, don't spend time in front of mirror, move straight onto the next step
Morning	Minimal self-care, sunscreen only	Defeated & deflated from negative self-talk	Don't allow myself to take care of my skin	Wash face, moisturise, sunscreen, one step after another, don't give myself time to dwell or criticise
Morning	Leave without breakfast	Avoidance & guilt	Leave the house without eating	Eat breakfast, pre-planned, non-negotiable
Morning	Bus to work	Body comparison	Focus on others & compare myself	Play a game on my phone, take a book to read

Now let's talk about some things you'll need to factor into your routine re-write…

What methods are you going to use to cope?

For example:

If you struggle with comparison on public transport, can you commit to playing a game on your phone or reading instead? Ask yourself, what would help me here?

If you struggle with lunchtimes at work, home, college, or university, can you schedule your lunch with someone you trust and ask them to help distract you during. If no one is available in person, can you instead make a deal with yourself, eat and call someone immediately after. Or would keeping your journal to hand help? You could use your Space to Cope to write out how you're feeling after.

If you are struggling to come up with new ways of coping or some positive distractions, don't worry, in the *Reflections* section which follows there is a whole series of prompts to work through and help you come up with some. If it is too challenging right now, feel free to put this section on pause and come back to it once you have completed the coping skills section.

What is your food and eating plan?

I realise how intense that question can feel, but I can't not mention it. You need some sort of strategy for tackling your food intake and how you're going to do it. Now, when I say plan, it doesn't have to be a specific "I will eat this exact meal' type of a plan, but it might be, depending on your requirements. When I use the word plan, what I mean is: *what is your intention or decision for addressing this area.* It could also be a 'plan' of committing to eating three meals a day, not skipping breakfast, eating freely or getting more specific with what you eat. We all have wildly different requirements, so I'll leave that with you to investigate, but please don't leave it out.

If you do need help in this area, I find it can help to break it down into two categories:

Do you need to address *what* you're going to eat; this is the *food* part, or do you need to address *how* you're going to eat; this is the *eating* part, or do you need help with both?

If it's both you could:

- Speak to your doctor for a referral to a dietician.

- Seek out a private dietician who specialises in eating disorder recovery and a non-diet approach.

- Seek out a private nutritionist who specialises in eating disorder recovery and a non-diet approach.

Now if you already know *what* to eat, but you're struggling to get through mealtimes and need support just in that area.

You could seek out help from:

- An eating disorder nutritional coach

- An eating disorder recovery coach

- An online meal support service

There are of course other services out there, this is by no means an exhaustive list, but I hope it can help to steer you in the right direction. Reading more on a non-diet approach in recovery and a holistic view of health can really help with mindset here too.

Once you've completed your routine re-write, it can be worthwhile to take it a step further and think about the more spontaneous situations which might occur in your life too. Routines are great, I've even grown to love refining mine *(as strange as that might sound)* however, it doesn't take into account, things such as a random work lunch or visiting family to celebrate a birthday. So, it can be worthwhile to take a few moments here to think about what they might be and come up with a plan.

Task: Step 1: Take a moment to identify any spontaneous activities or situations which may occur that might trigger disordered thoughts or behaviours.

I know this can feel uncomfortable, but this is about setting you up for success. What I find helpful here is to just think of your triggers as clues.

Ask yourself:

Outside of your everyday activities, when do you feel the need to engage in physically harmful behaviours?

Is there a particular situation which triggers them? Such as a work party, visiting relatives or a road trip?

Is there a person in your life that sets you off or even a group of people?

Are there topics of conversation you encounter that you find difficult to deal with?

Write down anything that comes to mind.

Task: Step 2: I want you to think about what you can do to intervene next time you feel yourself being triggered in the above situations and make a plan to challenge it.

Here are some questions to consider:

What could you use as a distraction in the moment?

Do you have someone you trust present in the situation to chat to?

If eating is involved, does it help to know what food will be available?

Can you prepare a mantra or affirmation to repeat to yourself at the time?

Will a particular breathing technique help, could you practice it beforehand?

Or can you avoid the situation all together?

I don't like to suggest making a habit of avoiding things, practicing social situations is essential in recovery. However, in the early stages, looking after yourself and protecting your energy comes first and foremost. It's okay to take a pass on events or certain people until you're feeling in a stronger frame of mind to deal with them.

I'll tell you a little story here...

When I first started out in recovery, I found whenever I met up with a particular university acquaintance, I always left the situation feeling bad about myself. Previously a lot of our conversation had focused on dieting, so it was only natural that they continued that conversation.

When I did tell them of my eating disorder, they didn't really get it. I gave it a couple of tries but the conversation didn't change so I then purposefully lessened the amount of contact I had with them.

Sure, I could have gone one step further and explained how their behaviour was impacting me but truthfully, I didn't have the energy to tackle that conversation.

So, if you're feeling any shame or guilt around avoiding someone or keep taking a rain check on certain events, please don't. You have to do what is best for you and your recovery.

By the end of this section, you should have:

A solid daily routine blueprint to combat disordered behaviours and thoughts.

A list of spontaneous situations which might trigger your behaviours.

A plan for dealing with those situations.

Handy hint: Write out your new routine blueprint on a piece of paper and keep it to hand in your bedroom, then refer to it as you perform the steps each day. This takes the thought out of it and makes it easier to flow from one step to the next.

8
REFLECTIONS

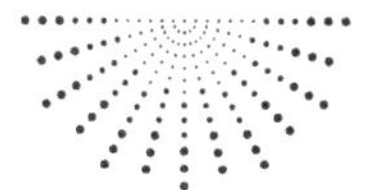

Now that you've re-written your routine, it's time to get back to some journaling. In this section I'm going to ask you to reflect on some important topics that typically come up in the early stages of recovery. The aim with these is to use your journal to explore your feelings on each topic.

Time wise, you can break up the prompts to suit you, but I suggest either choosing to do one of the prompts from the *Reflections* section each day or one section of the prompts each week.

For example: You could set yourself the goal of completing all the prompts in the social media section in a week, or you could do a question from the social media section each day which would give you nine days' worth.

The goal with this guide is to slowly work through each prompt. To let things sink in and give your mind and body time to focus, reflect and heal. If you try to rush through them hoping it will help you to get better faster, you might find yourself feeling overwhelmed. Paced consistency is key here.

I would suggest completing your *Daily* section in a morning and to then do your *Reflections* prompts in the evening. That's because some of the prompts can be quite heavy and it might pose a very emotional start to the day. However, my main request here is that you complete them when you have the most time to sit quietly, process and reflect.

To get your thoughts and words flowing onto that page I'm going to start with a juicy topic, one I'm sure we all have a lot of feelings on...

Social media

If you are actively engaging in social media, now is the perfect time to do a review of your usage and its role in your recovery. If you're not currently active online and have no intentions of being so, feel free to skip this prompt and move onto the next topic.

Prompt: What draws you to check your social media?

Prompt: How does it make you feel when you go online?

Prompt: How does it make you feel afterward?

Prompt: What feelings do you take away from using it?

Prompt: Does it make you feel connected?

Prompt: Do you compare yourself with others? If so, what aspects do you compare?

Prompt: Does it impact your recovery? Is it a help or a hinderance?

Prompt: What are the pros and cons of using it whilst you recover?

Prompt: Is there anything you could do to improve your experience of social media?

After journaling through those prompts, I'm sure you have a better idea of the role it will *(or won't)* play in your recovery.

Despite its rap, I don't think social media is all bad. On one hand it provides us with connection. It can also be inspiring and provide us with support we might not be getting elsewhere. But on the other hand, it can be a source of detrimental comparison and keep us stuck in some of our negative behaviours. If you make the decision to continue using it whilst you recover, I highly recommend doing a clean out and to make it a big one. Look at all the accounts you're following and ask yourself:

Does this person help me stay on a path of recovery or do they hinder it?

I want to add that I think it's important to go online with intention. The endless scrolling loop can be both addictive and demotivating. I suggest if you are going to engage, set yourself time limits. Allocate time to going online. Don't just make it your go to. Your brain really needs time to rest in recovery and if it's being flooded with images and other people's opinions, that can make it difficult.

For those of you wondering how I dealt with it… well, I cleaned up the accounts I followed to a point but some I couldn't let go of even though I knew they were a source of comparison for me. A couple of months into my recovery *(in stage one)* I found myself struggling to engage in any kind of social media activity without it inducing feelings of 'not being good enough' so I took a break for a couple of months, and I must say it really did help me.

Ps – If you're worried about taking a break, I get it, but it doesn't mean it's off limits forever. During stage two I re-introduced it, had a proper clear out and made it part of my life again. You've got to do what's best for you and your recovery today.

Diagnosis

Even though you've probably known for some time that something wasn't right. Getting an ED diagnosis can bring up a host of different feelings. Part of you might accept it, part of you might reject it. Whatever it is, I invite you to explore the following prompts and write it out.

I just want to mention here, that if you're not in a position to get a diagnosis *(for whatever reason)*, you do not need a diagnosis to make a start with your recovery, to recover or to use this guide. If this set of prompts doesn't sit well with you, feel free to move onto the next section.

Prompts *(for those with a diagnosis)*

What does your diagnosis mean to you?

Is it something you acknowledge or is it something you feel resistance towards?

If there is resistance here, explore why?

If you do feel a lot of resistance, try reframing it and ask yourself: In what ways does my diagnosis help me?

Prompts *(for those not diagnosed)*

If you are awaiting an appointment, how do you feel about the process?

If you have not yet sought out a diagnosis or an appointment for one, do you feel resistance towards getting one? Where do you think that resistance stems from?

Will a diagnosis be a turning point for you? Or are you indifferent? Does it feel like a step forward? Or a path you don't really want to go down?

If you have a lot of hesitations around a diagnosis, ask yourself: In what ways could a diagnosis help me?

A diagnosis can mean different things to different people. Is it needed? No. Can it help? In my opinion, yes, potentially. Truthfully, I never thought much about what it would mean, but turns out it was really important for me to hear those words coming from a professional's mouth. That said, I still didn't gel with the diagnosis at the time, at the back of my mind I still thought nah that's not me, not really, I'm just really stressed right now *(yeah right!)* but overtime it did sink in and more importantly it did help.

My point is, if you're feeling conflicted around it, that's totally understandable. Let all those feelings out here. Write down the very thing you might be avoiding acknowledging. In all of this, the most important thing is that you're taking steps in the right direction for your recovery. I'm proud of you.

Practicing patience

Learning to practice patience and sit with the feeling of discomfort it can bring is a real challenge in this early stage of recovery. I know for me, I just wanted to feel better overnight and if that wasn't possible, I wanted an exact timeline and exact instructions on how to recover and a guarantee that I would. So, if you're feeling frustrated by the passage of time and how long things are taking, I want you to take a moment here and let it all out on the pages.

Prompt: How does being 'patient' make me feel? When I think about having 'patience' in my recovery, how do I feel?

Whatever it is, I want you to let it all out here. Then come back and we'll talk some more.

* * *

Feel better for getting that out? I hope so.

I want to share with you now what helped me work through my own discomfort of patience and that was a simple yet very important reframe: *I learnt to see time as my ally.*

Instead of constantly feeling at war with time and frustrated that I wasn't instantly recovered, I instead began to see time as a gift. I focused on the fact that I *had* time to recover, that I *had* time and an opportunity to change my life for the better.

I focused on each day of recovery and tried my very best to stay grounded in the moment. I reminded myself that every day counts. That those days add up to being recovered. Now you might question here, what about those 'bad' days, the ones where you feel your progress is at a standstill or like you've taken a step or even a leap backwards. Those days are all part of it. They still count, regardless of your feelings towards them. They are all part of the process. Give yourself permission for this to take time and know that you can never be 'behind' in your own life or your own recovery.

Prompt: How would it feel to take recovery one day at a time? How can I learn to see time as my ally? What can keep me grounded?

For example:

Learning to take recovery one day at a time would feel difficult but when I reframe and see time as my ally, it brings me a feeling of calm. I can keep myself grounded in the moment by focusing on my breath and noticing things in nature.

Ps – remember the 'box' breathing technique right from the very start? just before stage one? When those pangs of impatience come knocking this is a great one to help you stay grounded in the moment.

Take a deep breath in for four through your nose, pause for four at the top and then release out through your mouth for four.

Exploring compassion

Self-compassion will be a recurring theme in this guide and that's because it's a really important practice to learn in recovery *(and life in general)* plus it's really hard to recover without it. At this stage of recovery, we can start to explore it as a concept and figure out where you could be a little more compassionate towards yourself in your life. We won't get into the why of it now, and why showing yourself compassion might be a struggle, that's for much later on in stage three. For now, let's just ease into the subject…

Prompt: Do you see yourself as a compassionate person? What does being compassionate look like to you? How does the idea of self-compassion make you feel?

I'll give you an example of how I felt in this stage…

My example:

I see myself as a compassionate person. I care about people, animals and nature. Being compassionate to me means being kind and considerate of others. Helping them when they need it. Listening to people and their needs. The idea of self-compassion makes me feel uncomfortable, I feel like I need to 'earn' it.

It's not uncommon to feel like self-compassion is something that needs to be 'earned' or that others are more inherently deserving of it than you. It's sadly something I hear time and time again, so if this is ringing a bell with you, I invite you to consider for a moment: *What makes someone worthy of compassion?*

To help put things in perspective, I like to think of it like this…

Does a baby deserve compassion? *Yes! Most definitely.*

Does an older person in a retirement home deserve compassion? *Of course!*

So, to me that says, compassion doesn't have an age requirement. We've got both ends of the scale there. And yes, those populations are both typically vulnerable, but I bet you show your friends compassion when they're having a hard time, right?

Do your friends have to earn your compassion? *Not really, it's just part of being friends.*

Would a stranger who fell in the street deserve your compassion? *I'd say so, that could happen to anyone!*

Then why not you?

You don't need to answer that, it's purely rhetorical. But I want this to serve as an important reminder that: *There are not different standards for you.*

You are just as deserving of compassion as anyone else, and whilst I know it can be a real challenge to change our attitude towards ourselves, I want you to try and invite a little more kindness into your life and reserve it just for you!

With that in mind, let's move onto the next prompt...

Prompt: What are three ways you can show yourself more kindness and compassion?

For example:

When I feel stressed, instead of negatively labelling myself, instead I'm going to ask - What do I need in this moment?

If I feel a certain way, I'm going to try not to cast harsh judgments of myself.

I'm going to be kind to myself by allowing myself to rest when I need it.

Prompt: What is one expectation you have of yourself that you can stop pressuring yourself to meet? How would it feel to release some of that pressure?

I know, I know. You might be cringing at this one or want to instantly skip it, but I invite you to sit with it for a moment. However, if it feels too hard right now or like it doesn't apply, you can move onto the next one.

Now, this expectation or 'pressure' doesn't have to be related to your ed or recovery, it could be work related, study related, family related, a general life related thing.

Whatever it is, try starting with:

I am going to stop pressuring myself to...

I'll share my personal ones from my own recovery:

I am going to stop pressuring myself to have a meticulously clean home.

I am going to stop pressuring myself to always look a certain way.

I am going to stop pressuring myself to say the 'right' thing.

I am going to stop pressuring myself to please everyone.

Now take a deep breath in, pause for four and release. I hope you feel a sense of relief after getting those out.

Before we finish up this section, I want you to take a moment to celebrate you *(something that can feel a bit uncomfortable at first)* but the perfect way to show yourself some kindness today!

Prompt: What are three things you're good at? How do they make you feel?

I want you to write down absolutely anything that springs to mind here.

For example:

I'm a good friend and that makes me feel warm inside. I'm good at listening to people and that makes me feel useful. I'm good at organising and that makes me feel capable.

All this self-compassion talk leads perfectly into our next section *(almost like I planned it)* and that is all about coping. *Why are the two linked you might ask?* Well, it can be pretty hard to practice positive coping skills and strategies if we're not very compassionate towards ourselves. I think the two really go hand in hand.

If you're feeling ready, let's move on…

Coping skills

I recall somebody asking me one day, *how do you cope?* It wasn't in reference to my eating disorder; it was more rhetorical. The person asking the question was having a hard time and I just shook my head and replied *I don't know, you just do, I guess.*

It struck me then that never in my life had I thought about coping skills or how I coped. To me it wasn't an active thing that I had a choice in. Typically, a situation would happen, and I would just deal with it. In hindsight, often not well, I just muddled through, but I didn't really know any different.

Thing is, we don't really get taught *how* to cope.

Growing up, we watch the adults in our lives deal with situations in certain ways and we then tend to mirror them, be it consciously or not. As we enter adulthood, some of us develop great coping skills and some of us, not so much *(I was one of the latter).*

Regardless of your past, chances are that your eating disorder behaviours are now one of the main ways you cope. If you're shaking your head and thinking it's not the case, I hear you. Neither did I, I actually thought it was a bit ludicrous to suggest such a thing.

But I assure you, whether you link the two up or not, your ed behaviours are a way of dealing with something in your life which was or is traumatic, something which makes you unhappy, stressed, depressed or anxious *(or all of the above.)* The link doesn't have to be clear yet, that's not what matters right now. Right now, what matters is actively looking at your current coping skills, trying to figure out what they are and then assessing whether or not they serve you in a positive way.

The aim of these prompts is to get a better idea of how you cope and to build a set of positive coping skills that you can turn to in times of need.

Prompt: What do you think your current methods of coping are? What things do you do to cope with stress in your life? Is there an activity or person you turn to?

Prompt: Do you seek out support and communicate when you're feeling stressed to others? Or do you typically turn more inward?

Prompt: Growing up, how did the people around you cope with their problems?

Prompt: What feelings do you associate with coping? i.e., do you associate not being able to cope with weakness? Or do you feel like you always have to be strong?

Prompt: Do you have some things you like to do to alleviate stress? Are they relaxing? Are they an escape? Overall, do they make you feel better?

Prompt: Write out the ways you cope and then evaluate whether or not they are positive and supportive to your recovery.

Ask yourself, does this help me cope in a way which supports my mental and physical wellbeing?

If you're struggling with this one, re-frame the question and ask what behaviours or activities could help you in your recovery? What behaviours or activities would be unhelpful to you?

By now, I'm sure you're starting to realise I love a story and an example, so I've included a list of things that helped me cope and things that didn't based on my own stage one.

Things that helped me cope: *Journaling (of course), sleeping, watching YouTube in bed, listening to soothing meditation music but not actually meditating because it was too hard to concentrate, seeing friends, walking (and admiring nice houses on my walk), going to the local park, making to-do lists, taking care of my skin.*

Things that didn't help me cope: *Hiding myself away, drinking excessive alcohol, not eating, talking shit to myself, endlessly scrolling social media and comparing myself to other people, going to group exercise classes and comparing myself to others, going to the gym and doing the same routines that fuelled my disorder, overworking, not sleeping enough, wearing nothing but my oldest tracksuit pants and a giant (not cute) hoodie.*

Now, you might have noticed some of my things on the 'didn't help me cope' list were exercise related, seemingly positive coping skills… if you don't have an eating disorder. This list is really personal, so I invite you to go through your own in turn and ask whether or not you are engaging in your 'things to cope' for the right reasons.

If you're not sure, it comes back to the question, *does this activity help me cope in a way which supports my mental and physical wellbeing?* If the answer is no, then we need to work on replacing it with some things that do.

An important note on walking: I mention this as a positive in my recovery and often use it as an example throughout this guide. However, if you are in significant energy deficit and have been advised to rest or walking is not in the picture for you, please don't take my example as prescriptive advice, just replace it with another activity.

How to develop some new coping skills…

Task: Break down the different areas of your life and then think about the possible stressful situations which might occur.

For example:

Home

Potential stressors: mealtimes, mornings, night times, confrontation with parents, partner or housemates.

Work

Potential stressors: high workload, confrontation with colleagues, food talk.

Learning (college, university etc)

Potential stressors: exams, lunch times, presentations.

Social situations

Potential stressors: dining out, food talk, body talk.

Once you have those, make a list of positive coping skills and activities you can turn to if that stressor arises.

You can incorporate any current positive ones, like the ones you explored in the previous prompts and add in some new ones too.

For example:

Journaling (you know I love it)

Getting outdoors (another fave)

Listening to meditation music

Listening to podcasts

Laughing (have a go-to show which always makes you force out even just a smile)

Reading

Spending time with a pet (if you have one)

Skincare session (facemask etc)

Nap

Cross stitch (I tried this one, it wasn't for me)

Bear in mind, effective coping skills… things… habits *(whatever you want to call them)* should be something you'll actually use. It's no good thinking I'll meditate next time I feel panicked at home if meditation is not something you typically practice or at least have an interest in. I'm all for trying new things but they have to at the very least be desirable to you.

Once you have your list, you can assign them to each situation. Different habits work in different environments, hence why it's important to break them down into sections i.e., journaling is a great one for home, but not so much if you're out at work *(depending on your job of course)*.

For example:

If I'm at home and become stressed at mealtimes I will put on a podcast (obviously depends on who you live with).

If I'm at home and become stressed with my housemate(s) I will take myself outdoors and go for a walk (daytime, good weather version).

Evening (winter version) If I'm at home and become stressed with my housemate(s) I will call one of my friends or cosy up in bed and watch a tv show that makes me laugh.

If I'm studying for exams and become stressed (inevitable) I will take a nap (if I'm home) or if I'm at the university library, I'll go find a friend to talk to or take a break for a walk.

If writing them out in this format doesn't work for you, do as I have and create a table.

Time of day	Location	Situation	Coping method
Mealtimes	Home	Feeling stressed at mealtimes	Put on a podcast, Play a phone game, Journal
Daytime (Summer)	Home	Conflict with housemate	Take myself outdoors and go for walk, Pay extra attention to the trees & birds
Evening (Winter)	Home	Conflict with housemate	Call a friend or cosy up in bed and watch a tv show that makes me laugh
Morning	University library	Studying for exams	Go find a friend on campus to talk to or schedule study with a friend

I hope after this exercise you have a solid list of things to turn to in all the different areas of your life.

Next up, we're going to talk about a topic which I think goes hand in hand with coping and that is... communication.

Here's why...

If you can't communicate what is happening with you or feel you're not able to, you typically turn inward to cope. Now, that can be okay, I'm sure after the previous task you have some really great things to turn to, however, if we regularly avoid communicating what's going on with us, we miss out on a lot of potential social support which can be an absolute lifesaver in recovery... therefore it's time for...

Difficult conversations

Telling people in our lives about the issues we've been facing can feel really overwhelming. It took me a long time to build up the courage to do this, so if you are struggling, I hear you, it's completely understandable. However, telling people will help you to step away from any shame your ed might be holding over your head which ultimately will help you progress in your recovery and that's what we want.

If you haven't told anyone about what's going on with you yet or are putting off telling certain people, I've got some prompts to help you plan for those conversations.

But, if you have told people and this section doesn't feel like something you need to work through, feel free to move on to the next one.

For those that haven't told anyone or are putting off telling certain people, let's get into it...

Prompt: What is your fear around telling people? What are you afraid they will think? Is it that they won't understand? Is it that they won't be accepting? Whatever it is, let it out here.

Prompt: What do you want to tell people? How do you want them to support you? Do you need anything from them or are you telling them as a step of commitment to your recovery?

Prompt: Is there someone in particular that you're worried about telling? Why are you worried about telling them? Write out all the things you want to say to that person here. You can write it in the form of a letter, a speech or just put down some thoughts on the pages.

Ask yourself, will this person be receptive? If not, will sharing with them help my recovery?

If you feel like having a conversation with this person will do more harm to you than good, don't feel you have to share with them. You don't have to tell everyone in your life, though I encourage you to at least tell a few people.

It's time to move on to your last but not least reflection for stage one…

Body checking & other checking behaviours

Is bodychecking part of your day? How about any other checking behaviours? Now I'm not talking about glancing at your reflection in the mirror before you head out or checking the door is locked one time before you go out for the day. That's regular behaviour. I'm talking about the kind where you scrutinise yourself in the mirror multiple times a day or have to go back and repeatedly check if things are locked, switched off or in place.

If so, it's time to explore…

Prompt: How does body checking, or any checking behaviour make you feel? Is it helpful? Is it harmful? Does it influence your mood?

Prompt: Are you conscious of your checking or does it feel more like a compulsion? i.e., something you automatically find yourself doing without actively thinking.

Prompt: What feeling do you hope that checking will fulfil?

Prompt: Next time you feel the urge to check, could you stop yourself? If not, why not?

First, I just want to say that these behaviours can be really tough to let go of, so don't be hard on yourself if it is a struggle to overcome them.

For those of you finding letting go of a checking habit a challenge, give the task below a try:

Task: Keep a tally of how many times a day you bodycheck or engage in another type of checking behaviour *(I recommend using your phone notes here)* and then try to reduce the number of times you check by one each day.

For example:

If you checked x number of times on Monday, I want you to tell yourself that on Tuesday, you have to reduce that number by one. Once you reach your limit that day, you have to then commit to no more checking that day. Then on Wednesday, you bring that number down again by one and repeat for each day that follows.

* * *

Guess what? You've worked through all of the *Reflections* for stage one!

Congratulations! That's a huge achievement! There was a lot to work through, but I hope you found it really beneficial.

Now remember to keep going with your *Space to Cope* and *Daily* journal entries until you feel you're ready to move on to the next stage.

You might be questioning, *but how do I know when that is?* And the answer is, it's a very personal choice but in case you're struggling to figure out when that is for you, I've made the following table to act as a rough guide. But remember it's only a guide! Listen to yourself first and foremost.

Throughout Stage 1	Ready to move to Stage 2 when...	Throughout Stage 2	Ready to move to Stage 3 when...	By the end of Stage 3
Fighting the constant urge to binge, purge, restrict.	You might still have urges, but you are no longer acting upon them each time.	You're eating more freely but still dealing with the mental aspects around food. Urges lessening.	Challenging and overcoming the mental aspects of food and eating behaviours. Urges lessening.	Maintaining positive physical habits and not engaging in any harmful behaviours. Urges ceased.
Fear of eating & food measurements (calories, macros etc.)	Managing to eat more regular meals, not feeling as controlled by food measurements.	No longer feeling out of control around food, significant trust regained. Not feeling the need to measure foods.	Still not feeling out of control around food, trust remains. Not feeling the need to measure foods.	Eating freely. Food sits in proper perspective in your life and does not dominate it.
Frequent moods swings & heightened emotions.	Moods growing more stable, though still a lot of emotional ups and downs.	Feeling more emotionally stable. Maintaining healthy relationships with those around you.	Generally, feel good but still like you're searching for the last piece of the puzzle but you're not sure what it is (cryptic I know).	Feeling positive about the future, strong and stable in your recovery.
Fighting the urge to over exercise.	Exercise might still feel problematic.	Challenging your relationship with moving your body.	Learning to move your body from a place of love and not fear or punishment.	Moving your body from a place of love.
Constant bodychecking. (Only if this is a feature for you)	Bodychecking lessening.	Bodychecking ideally ceased.	Growing acceptance of your body.	Accepting and appreciative of your body.

9
STAGE TWO

QUESTIONING BELIEFS

"When things change inside you, things change around you." - Unknown.

Prerequisite: Completion of stage one

Your goal: To maintain new habits and improve your understanding of yourself.

First up, I just want to say a massive congratulations to you on completing stage one. I'm so incredibly proud of you right now. Your commitment to your recovery speaks for itself. You're showing up, doing the work, and improving your life every day. How fantastic is that?

I'm sure your overall mood has improved since you started. I'm guessing your thinking is a bit clearer too, but you're still probably dealing with a lot of emotional ups and downs. That's only natural given all the changes you've been making. You can't be expected to be on cloud nine at all times. Recovery is tough, but you being here, suggests to me that you're a whole lot tougher.

Now that your harmful physical behaviours have lessened, you're in a better position to start tackling some of the mental aspects of your ed. In this stage we're going to start questioning a lot of the thoughts and feelings you might be having and address the beliefs which underpin them too.

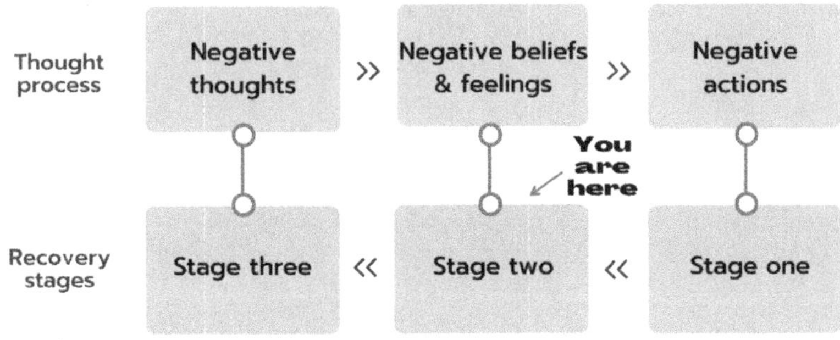

How you're going to get there…

You're going to start out with a review of all the great things you've accomplished so far, check in with how you're feeling and if your routine is still working for you. Then you're going to start reflecting.

I want to forewarn you that I'm going to ask you to query a range of topics including some on body image and a lot on food behaviour. Now I know some of these will be really challenging and I will always endeavour to be both sensitive and responsible in my discussions of them. But I want you to know that addressing and unpacking all of these things is what will keep you going with your recovery for the long term.

If you're reading this and thinking that it sounds really intense and you're not sure you're ready, feel free to read ahead, scan over some of the prompts and make an assessment based on that. If it is too confronting, you can always return to stage one and repeat the *Daily* section for a while until you feel more ready.

My personal experience of this stage was that the return of more 'normal' eating patterns had brought many positives to my life, but I was still very much battling with the mental aspects of my ed.

In this stage it is common to find that as your eating improves and your exposure to different food related situations increases, a lot of shame and guilt can crop up. You might be dealing with body changes too and that can feel overwhelming, so please be gentle with yourself.

What is the suggested timeframe?

You can do a prompt every day or pick an area to focus on each week. Go at whatever pace feels right for you. There is no right and wrong. This is *your* recovery.

The Recover You Journaling Method.

Important, don't skip this one

New stage, same structure, but with a few tweaks and some very different topics. As you know, there are five journal sections which make up the RYJM, and each serves a different purpose:

Space to Cope

This is the exact same as before. A section of blank pages in your journal to come to if you're feeling overwhelmed. My hope is that you won't need to use it as much in this stage but please do if you need it.

Daily

I'm going to give you choices with this section this time around.

You can either continue to complete the *Daily* section *(check-in, affirmations, gratitude)* each day or, not bother with it and choose to do one of the prompts from the *Reflections* section each day.

Another option is to do both. If you do want to do both, I would suggest completing the *Daily* section in a morning and then do a *Reflections* prompt in the evening.

Now I say this because the prompts are kind of heavy, there might be a lot for you to unpack and it could pose a very emotional start to the day. Just something to keep in mind.

Headspace

In stage two, this section is where you'll reflect on the progress you've made in your recovery so far, address any concerns you're having and celebrate your accomplishments too!

Routine

This time around you're going to review your routine and tweak where needed.

Reflections

This section is made up of journal prompts. In this stage we dive a little deeper than we have before.

10
HEADSPACE

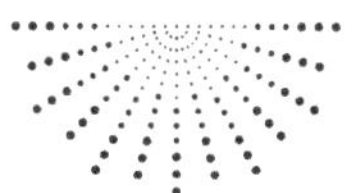

It's time to do a little review of the changes you've made since starting out in stage one. Does it feel like you've come so far? Well let me tell you, you have! Even if it doesn't seem like it right now, I assure you, all of the changes you are making will add up over time to make an enormous difference to your life.

Prompt: When you think about the changes you've made since starting out in stage one, what things spring to mind?

How are you feeling about them?

What are the most significant changes to you?

Prompt: Thinking about the different areas of your life. How have the changes you've made impacted your personal life and relationships?

Have those changes impacted your work or career plans positively?

How has each area of your life changed?

Write out everything that comes to mind.

My example:

My recovery positives so far have been feeling more present, feeling physically better and not as panicked too, that's been a huge bonus. I've been sleeping better. My general mood is better too. I've been out to restaurants a few times and enjoyed myself mostly. Sometimes I do find it a struggle not to panic at the menu, but I know it will get better over time. I've found I have more focus for my studies which has been helpful as I'm in my final year.

Now I just want to say that if you've made all these positive changes and you don't really feel great about them or as good as you expected, that is perfectly okay. This is a space to validate all of your feelings. Whatever they may be. You don't have to be feeling all rosy about everything, all the time, but if you are, that's fantastic! I'm so glad.

Recovery can be a bit of an emotional rollercoaster so give yourself permission to feel all the feels! You don't have to pretend everything is amazing. You can still make progress and have conflicted feelings.

Prompt: It's time to dig out your WHY from stage one or maybe by now you know it off by heart.

Once you have it to hand, ask yourself if it still stands?

Is this still WHY you want to recover? If it is, leave it as is and move on. If you feel like you want to add another layer to it, go ahead.

For example:

My original WHY was - I want to be present in my relationships and enjoy my life.

Looking back, I think I'd add in something about my body.

My WHY 2.0:

I want to be present in my relationships, enjoy my life and appreciate my body.

I added the part about my body because as I recovered, I realised that I had spent so many years hating on it that I didn't appreciate all that it did and does for me.

Before we move forward. I want you to check in with yourself here. I know we did that a bit in the first prompt, but this is a bit more general.

Prompt: What's on your mind? Are there certain things about recovery troubling you? or are you feeling pretty darn good and ready to get cracking with some more prompts?

You can be pleased about your recovery but still have hesitations and old thoughts and feelings that keep cropping up. I know I did so if you do too, now's your chance to get them out. Anything that's on your mind. Let it out here.

For me in this stage, I felt angry at some people in my life and their lack of awareness around what I was going through. I still took it very personally when someone spoke about calories, weight change or some ridiculous diet in front of me *(I promise you, if you do the work, that will change overtime. Now it doesn't bother me whatsoever)*. I've let go of that anger too. I now see that it's really hard for people in our life to get what we're going through.

In this stage, I also worried a lot that I would never feel better about myself. I knew I was doing the right thing, but I felt a bit lost in life *(if you do too, fear not, we're going to do a whole bunch of prompts on that sort of thing).*

Recovery is a process. I really want to reiterate that. We have to ride the waves. The ups and downs. I thought I would be instantly happy once I stopped with my physically damaging behaviours and truthfully, I was some days and then others it just felt really hard and a constant battle. But my WHY kept me going, my journal kept me going.

Really use those pages to cope. To get it all out. And talk, if you can and have someone you trust, tell them. They might not completely understand but I know they'll meet you with kindness and love.

After a couple of potentially very emotional prompts, we need to finish our *Headspace* on a high. Time to switch gears and…

Prompt: Name one accomplishment you are really proud of in your recovery so far. What's the major one?

Write it down. Then come back here.

Read whatever you've written back to yourself. Now go to your nearest mirror. Look at your reflection, give yourself a high five and say: *I am proud of myself. I have...* *insert accomplishment here*

I know it might sound like a really cheesy thing to do but I recently read the High 5 Habit created by Mel Robbins and there is actual science to support the benefits of giving yourself a high five in the mirror! Apparently, the unexpected act of high fiving yourself puts your brain on high alert and makes it pay extra attention to the message you're repeating! How cool is that? I've been doing it each morning and I do find it to be a mood boost so if you feel so inclined, give it a try.

And know that I'm always here cheering you on and sending you a high five too! I'm so proud of you and your commitment to your recovery. Now, let's get into routines…

11
ROUTINE

Remember how you reviewed your routine in stage one and changed things up to better support you? Well, how's it been going? Is your routine still working for you? Have any other problematic areas cropped up?

This is a great time to do a mini review. Your routine is crucial in making recovery work for the long haul.

Prompt: Is there a particular time of day where I still struggle to overcome disordered behaviours or thoughts? What could I do differently to combat them?

For example:

If you're struggling after dinner, could you ask someone you live with to go on a walk with you or play a game? If you live alone, could you organise to meet someone after dinner for that walk? (If walking is not in the picture for you, switch it out for something else)

What could you do to help set yourself up for success?

For me in stage two, I'd stopped with the physically harmful behaviours, but I still had strong urges after dinner which I would combat by getting out the house and going on a walk or having a tv show lined up to watch straight after. I found too much free time in the evenings a struggle, so I focused on finding new enjoyable things to do to distract myself. And eventually, over time, those new habits and activities stuck, and I said goodbye to the urges.

Take this time to give your routine a once over before you head into *Reflections*.

12

REFLECTIONS

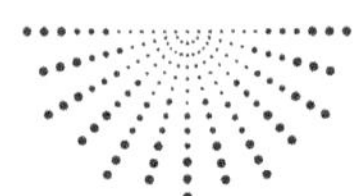

Now you've addressed your *Headspace* and *Routine* it's time to get into your *Reflections.* In this stage you're going to be doing a lot more of these than you did in stage one. This is because you've tackled the 'actions' aspect of your eating disorder and now, you're going to explore the things that precede it *(remember the diagram.)*

I want to give you a bit of a heads up here. I am going to talk about and ask that you explore some potentially upsetting topics such as your relationship with food and your body. I want you to know that whenever I ask you to do anything like this, I am only ever coming from a place of love. I want you to feel better, I want you to recover, and stay recovered more than anything and for that, I truly believe that you have to work through some difficult questions and challenge a lot of the beliefs you might hold.

I want you to know that everything that I've included in this guide I have thought about extensively and worked through myself. In fact, I've included a lot of my answers to the prompts based on my mindset at the time. If you feel completely different, that's only natural. We're all different. I just share my answers, so you know how someone else going through these stages felt. Your answers are inside of you! And I hope this guide helps to draw them out, gives you some things to think on and helps you to heal.

Ps - If you find yourself thinking this is too much. Come back to it another day. There is no rush to get through any of the prompts here.

Current food feelings

We all walk different paths in life, and we all face different issues in our recovery. These are some of the things I questioned in order to start my process of healing and some common themes that crop up in recovery. I acknowledge that they might not always be the same things you're facing but I invite you to give those that resonate with you a try.

Prompt: In this moment, what does food and eating mean to you?

I realise this prompt can bring up a lot of mixed feelings, so take your time with it, focus on taking some nice deep breaths in and out, then just write out whatever comes to mind.

Prompt: What positive things does an adequate balanced food intake bring to my life?

This could be anything from more energy and concentration to better balanced hormones. Whatever it is, take a moment to really focus on the positive here.

Prompt: How do you feel when people bring up the subject of food around you?

The idea of this prompt is to feel into where you're at with this and be really honest with yourself. It's another chance to validate your feelings. If you're angry with people for speaking insensitively around you, write it out here. If you're not fussed, write that out too. It's a space to let it all out.

Prompt: Has your attitude towards food changed?

If it's still a struggle to think about this subject. Write that out too. And ask yourself, *why?*

Prompt: How do you find mealtimes? Is one time of day more of a challenge than others?

Prompt: How do you find eating in front of others?

I just wanted to write a note on this one. If you're struggling to eat in front of people, you're not alone. This one still rears its head for me from time to time.

If you do have fears around it, it's a good idea to write them down.

For example: If you have a family member that might comment on what you are eating. Write out the imagined conversation here.

I find that once you put it down on paper it helps to lessen its power.

Some thoughts on food talk at mealtimes...

People often have no idea how to act around someone with an eating disorder. Plus, in general, people often comment on a lot of food and eating behaviours of others *(that they shouldn't)* because that's a thing in our society. Doesn't mean it's okay, but to say it doesn't happen would be glossing over the truth.

If you are faced with issues around food talk and eating comments at mealtimes, I like to think there are two ways you can tackle it.

One, you can call them out on it.

Two, you can ignore it.

I've used both approaches depending on the situation…

An example of one in action:

I went out with some friends for dinner about six months into recovery. One of them started talking about how 'bad' they had been food wise, going on and on (I now know the whole concept of food being bad and good is bs, but more on that later). I used to be part of this conversation too, I would join in, so I see why they thought it was okay to talk in that way. However, I chose to address it because I know my friends would be receptive to what I had to say. I reminded them of my eating disorder and said I'd rather not talk about this sort of thing anymore. It made things a bit awkward in the moment but nothing devastating happened. I am still friends with those people today and it hasn't negatively impacted our friendship whatsoever.

An example of two in action:

Nearly a year into recovery I recall going out for a dinner with family members and somebody commented on my choice to eat a dessert. In the moment I felt that sting, that panic, my brain wanted to spiral. But instead, I paused, took a deep breath, and considered the situation for a moment, then chose to simply ignore it. I just acted like it didn't exist. Thing is, some older people in my life really don't get eating disorders. I could explain it over and over, but it just wouldn't sink in. When my response is a polite nod or silence, ultimately, it's more awkward for them than it is for me.

I feared so deeply the first time this would happen. I felt like I would burst into flames if anyone commented on my eating, but through writing it out and exposing myself to various situations,

I've learnt that I am stronger than that. And I know that you are too.

Prompt: I invite you to write out any fears around food talk and ask yourself, is this one comment going to stop me from living out my WHY?

Prompt: How do you feel eating in public say at a restaurant or café?

Prompt: If you are responsible for cooking in your home, how are you finding it? If you are responsible for the supermarket shopping, how are you finding it?

A word *(or two)* on this. I found both of these a real challenge. It felt like I had forgotten how to cook, and I found it a real struggle to put a meal together or shop for groceries without feeling overwhelmed. In the end, I tried one of those meal delivery kits and that did alleviate some of the pressure. So, if it is within your budget and this is something you struggle with, it might be worth a try.

Prompt: How do you feel about attending events where there is food? Such as a work party or a family gathering.

Remember your list of coping skills from stage one? Have you been putting them into action here?

Prompt: What role does food currently play in your life? Has this role changed since stage one?

Health & Movement

Prompt: What does health mean to you? What's the first thing that comes to mind? What does being 'healthy' mean to you?

If you find yourself shaking your head because you don't know why I've included this or where to even start.

Ask yourself, *what feelings do these questions of health trigger?*

I realise this might seem like a bit of an odd one, but I pose this question because we *(as a society)* often have a very limited view of what health is. We tie it back to just the physical aspects and it is so much more than that. It encompasses our mental and spiritual wellbeing, even our environment and social needs too.

In my own recovery, as I moved away from the thinking of health solely being a physical thing and started to ensure I was looking after other aspects of my health too, I found that it really helped my mindset.

Prompt: I invite you to explore what health looks like for you today and moving forward.

Ask yourself:

Is my environment supportive of my recovery?

Do I feel supported in my recovery?

If not, would I consider joining a local or online support group?

What does being spiritual mean to me? Is it something which resonates, or not really?

Am I meeting my mental health needs?

Do I need to dedicate more time to an activity which could benefit them?

Do I need to rest more?

Prompt: What does exercise mean to you? How does the word exercise make you feel?

Prompt: If you are exercising, why do you do it? Do you enjoy it, or do you feel obligated to?

Prompt: What outcome do you attach to exercise, if any?

I'm so sorry if you wince at this word. I still do! But I think it's important to think about it and be clear with how it's making you feel. When we get really clear on something and our feelings around it, we can make the adjustments needed.

I'm going to be honest with you, my brain still associates the word exercise with guilt even after all this time. I still feel a twinge. I actually prefer to call it movement *(hence the title of this section)* or moving my body or even a workout. To me those terms are less emotionally loaded.

Now if you're reading this thinking, I'm good with exercise. I'm happy calling it that and don't feel I have a negative relationship with it. Great! I'm so glad. Feel free to head on into the next section. However, if it's something you're struggling with I'll share my story below so you can get an idea of how it went for me.

My story

Let me preface this by saying I was a chronic over exerciser, the idea of not going to the gym filled me with panic. When I started out in stage one, I still tried to do my usual gym routine, because I couldn't imagine my life without it. Thing is, it only perpetuated my ed mindset. So, I thought, I'll just do yoga at the gym instead. But every time I went, I felt like a failure for not doing my full gym routine. The place was full of reminders. And truly, it brought out the worst in me. Before I knew it, I was hitting the gym pre-yoga. It was not helping anyone. I remembered reading a recovery story and they said that *you can't be expected to heal in the same environment that you got sick.* That really hit home, I knew what I needed to do.

I cancelled my gym membership and from that day forward I stuck to walking. Instead of fixating on the screen of a gym machine, I would pay extra attention to all of the things on my walk. Look at trees, notice their leaves. Try to listen out for birds *(tricky in a city! but doable).* Truthfully, some days I was filled with sadness on those walks, like I needed to be working harder, but I kept going out regardless because I knew deep down that I would never have the breakthrough I needed whilst I continued with my same old routines. To this day, walking is still one of my favourite things to do. I still don't go to the gym. I've tried going back several times over the years, but I don't particularly enjoy it anymore. I've found I prefer to get my movement in, in different ways. That's not to say I will never set foot in a gym again in my life, but I will never do it to compensate, punish or berate myself. That's the big difference.

Now, I'm not dictating to you here what you should or shouldn't do but I just want you to think about what I've said. If you're still doing your same exercise routines, ask yourself: *is this truly helping my recovery? Is it truly helping my mind and body to heal?*

If you find yourself answering no, then try to cut back. You don't have to stop entirely but just start reducing how much you do a little at a time. Then maybe switch things up and try some different activities to get your body moving. I get how scary all of the above can feel, but trust me, overtime, you'll thank yourself for addressing it now.

Prompt: What would it mean to change your routine? What would it mean to slow things down a little?

Comparison

You've probably heard it said before but there's a reason it sticks around and that's because comparison really is the thief of joy. Now, I do want to acknowledge here that humans by their very nature are geared to compare, it's a survival thing. And not all comparisons are bad, sometimes they inspire you to implement positive changes or give you little hints about what you actually want in life.

However, engaging in negative comparison can be a prominent feature when living with an eating disorder. I know for me; it was a significant issue. I would spend countless hours comparing every aspect of my very being to others and to past versions of myself too. These thoughts of comparison ran on a constant loop in my head. It was exhausting. So, if you're nodding your head thinking *'yup, me too'*, know that I've been there. I get it. Now, what I found helpful was to first bring awareness to the comparison. To get clear on when I was engaging in comparison, what I was comparing, and what feeling it was giving me. So we'll start with that and then I have a task to help you break the cycle.

Let's get into it…

Prompt: In what ways do you compare yourself to others? What are your areas of comparison?

Prompt: What situations trigger thoughts of comparison for you?

Once you have that, I want you to explore the following…

Prompt: Is your comparison typically positive in nature or typically negative?

Prompt: What feelings do you get when you compare yourself to others?

Prompt: What do you think achieving these things would bring to your life? Are they things you actually care about or want? Are those things supportive of your recovery?

Task: Next time you catch yourself engaging in comparison, be it comparing yourself with another person or a past version of you, I want you to try and catch those thoughts and ask: *is this something I want? Is it supportive of my recovery?*

If the answer to both questions is yes, then by all means, write it down, make it a goal for the future.

But if the answer to the last one is no, then ditch it immediately! It goes in the rubbish; it goes in your mental trash can.

For example:

Say you're on public transport and start to compare the condition of your hair with others (I realise it might sound odd, but it's something I used to do)

The comparison happens, the negative self-talk starts up. Catch yourself!

Ask yourself: is this something I want? (Yes, feels that way)

Is it supportive of my recovery? (Somewhat, the negative thoughts aren't, but they tell me I'd quite like to get my hair done or at least take better care of it)

Action: Buy myself a hair mask

Another example:

Say you're on social media and start to compare your body with others.

Ask yourself: is this something I want? (Yes. It might well feel like you do in that moment)

Is it supportive of my recovery? No! Then it goes in the mental trash can!

Get the idea?

For all the things that are not supportive of your recovery, I want you to try your best to mentally ditch them and start to believe in you and all the weird, wonderful things that make you, you!

Your journey through life is unique.
Your journey through recovery is unique.
And you are unique.
And that is something to be celebrated.

Prompt: What are three unique aspects of yourself that you are grateful for?

For example:

I am grateful for my sense of humour, I am grateful for my planning skills, I am grateful for my creativity.

Body Image, Confidence & You

I feel this section needs no introduction, so let's get straight into it.

I want you to take a deep breath in through your nose, hold for four and release out through your mouth.

You're ready.

Prompt: What feelings do you associate with your body?

Prompt: Finish this sentence… I am *or* my body is…

Do you typically gravitate towards the positive or the negative here?

Prompt: How do you feel about your appearance?

Prompt: What is one thing you appreciate about your body?

Prompt: How do you feel about your body changes?

Prompt: Your body helps you to move through the world, but it's not all that you are. Write out a list of the things that make you, you! It can help here to think about what you want people in the world to know about you.

For example: I have a great knowledge of music. I am really organised and messy at the same time. I have a great memory for faces, but not so much for names.

Whatever unique things that make you, you! I want you to take a moment to write them down here.

Prompt: How do you feel about yourself? What do you appreciate about yourself? I want you to consider all aspects of you here.

Prompt: What are your strengths in friendships and relationships?

Prompt: What do you like most about your personality?

Prompt: Which areas of your life are you confident in? Which areas do you feel capable in? Which areas do you not feel confident in?

If you're not sure, think about the areas of your life where you feel free to be yourself.

Which areas do you feel like your opinion is valued? Which areas do you feel like you have a voice?

Go through the different areas of your life and write out if you feel confident in them or not and the reasons why.

For example:

Work: Confident (feel like I know what I'm doing and that my opinion is respected.)

Social life: Confident (feel like I have good friends, love making them laugh.)

Family: Nup (feel like my opinion is never respected, like I'm the baby regardless of my age.)

Finances: Not really (feel like my finances are something I don't want to think about.)

Study: Not really (feel like I have to push that bit harder than everyone else.)

Prompt: For the areas of your life that you are confident in, could you transfer some of that energy and attitude to your more unconfident areas? If not, why not?

What are your beliefs in your unconfident areas of your life?

How could you overcome them?

For example:

Finances: My beliefs in this area come from my past history of debt. I acknowledge that I'm better now but still feel those old labels live with me. When I look at my confidence in other areas of my life, I realise that I am capable of change, and I am capable of improving my relationship with money.

You might be wondering why am I getting you to write about confidence. Well, that's because it tends to overlap with our self-esteem and that is something which is typically low in people with eating disorders.

What's the difference between the two? Well, self-esteem is how much you appreciate and value yourself and self-confidence is how much you believe in yourself and your abilities. I figure we can't expect to boost one without examining the other.

Prompt: Looking at the previous prompts you've written on confidence and your feelings about yourself, where does your validation tend to come from?

Is it mainly based on internal factors and sources? Or is it based on external factors and sources?

In what areas of your life do you feel validated? How does that make you feel?

For example:

Internal factors and sources: encouraging yourself, prioritising your feelings, acknowledging your strengths, treating yourself with kindness, accepting all parts of yourself.

External factors and sources: other people complimenting or praising you, likes on a social media post, any academic, financial or career success that is measured by external milestones.

I'm going to take a wild guess here and say that a lot of your validation probably comes from external sources. It tends to be the main source for most of us. However, something we often overlook is the power to validate ourselves. I say overlook, but it's not like we're ever taught to do it. But today is different! Yup. It's time to learn some things you can do to validate yourself.

And why is that so important? Well, if our self-esteem and confidence continue to be based on external factors, the goalposts are constantly moving and we're not in charge. Learning how to self-validate takes back that power and helps us to be the ones in control of how we feel about ourselves and our abilities.

How to self-validate…

First up, get to know yourself, your feelings and what you need. Your journal is a great way of doing this. Get into the habit of asking yourself, *what do I need right now? How can my needs be met in this moment? What can I do to meet them?*

Secondly, practice accepting your feelings and needs without passing judgement. I find that responding to yourself the same way you would respond to a friend is a great way of doing this.

Next up, learn to celebrate your accomplishments. Don't wait for others to congratulate you. Be the first to tell yourself you did a great job and take time out to celebrate your wins.

And finally, design yourself some personalised validating affirmations. By now you know I love an affirmation!

Here's some to get you started:

I am capable and worthy of achieving my goals
I am worthy as I am with no conditions attached
I am worthy of love and respect, I will not settle for anything less
My worth isn't based on others approval
I am confident in my own worth and value
I am doing my best and learning every day
I am grateful for all that I have and all that I am

I allow myself to feel without judgement
I believe in myself and my abilities
I am proud of myself

Let's finish this section with one final prompt.

Prompt: Write down three things you like about yourself.

I like...

Identity

It's very common to feel a loss of identity in recovery. I know I certainly did. In truth, I wasn't sure who I was without my disorder. Looking back, I can see that my eating disorder had replaced any hobbies I previously had in my life. Any free time was taken up by something related to it. It wasn't like I consciously did that, it just happened over time and once I stopped with the physically damaging behaviours *(which was great)* I had time and energy to pour into something else, but I had no idea what that would be.

During this stage it's perfectly natural to feel a whole bunch of mixed feelings about what's going on and the changes being made. I personally experienced a sense of loss, at times I felt numb and confused and honestly it shocked me. I'd expected to feel so much better, all the time. And some days I did. But some days I felt completely lost. I'm being honest here, because if you're in that space, I want you to know that you can and will come out the other side. We have made huge changes to our life, and yes, they're changes for the better, but sometimes in can feel rough (*kind of like a relationship breakup).*

With that in mind, I invite you to explore the next prompt...

Prompt: Do you feel lost without your disorder, are you starting to feel free, or is it a combination of both?

If you're not feeling any sense of loss, I'm so glad! You can feel free to skip this next prompt as it might not resonate.

Prompt: Use this space in your journal to acknowledge your eating disorder and the impact it had and continues to have on you.

Add in anything you feel you miss and any feelings of loss surrounding your eating disorder. This is a space to validate your feelings. To admit what you're feeling.

For example: My eating disorder ruled my life. When I think back to those days in the depths of it, I feel sad for myself. I'm glad I'm getting better and that's why I feel so confused because I am happy about it but some days I feel really lost.

Take a big deep breath in and out. I hope you feel a sense of relief after sharing that.

Next, I want you to start to get curious and think about: *who am I without it? Who was I before it and who do I want to be?*

Prompt: What are your five core values? What does each one mean to you?

If you're struggling for inspiration here, I've created a list of core values for you, just head on over to the Recover You website and you'll find it there.

For example:

My five core values are: Communication, Freedom, Understanding, Kindness, and Connection.

To me communication means using my voice and speaking up for myself. It means working through and verbalising my feelings etc.

Prompt: Who do you want to show up in the world as? What do you care about? What are your strengths?

Prompt: How can you start to invite a little more joy into your life?

At this point of recovery, it can be a great idea to start thinking about some new things you can introduce or re-introduce to your life. This is the ideal time to try out some new hobbies. You don't have to go all out but if you want to, go for it!

Guilt & Shame

As you begin to eat more freely, it can be common for guilty thoughts around food to intensify. Chances are you've been telling yourself that certain foods are forbidden for such a long time, that of course your brain is going to hit the wtf button when you eat it. On one hand, this means you're making progress and that is absolutely fantastic. I'm so proud of you! However, I am well aware of the mental battle that can surface during this time.

If you're finding yourself thinking, *I shouldn't have eaten that or I feel so bad for eating x y z, I'm bad for eating x y z etc*, it's time to start unpacking that.

As uncomfortable as it might be, I invite you to first sit with that feeling of guilt for a moment and explore it a little on the pages…

Prompt: When feelings of guilt arise, how do they feel? How do they feel in your body? What do they make you think?

Prompt: What does this feeling of guilt give you? What does this feeling of guilt take from you?

Prompt: If you could live the day free from guilt tomorrow, how would that feel?

Take a deep breath in and sigh it out.

I realise that's pretty heavy stuff to work through. I'm proud of you.

Next up, I want to talk about something which can lead to that guilt…

Time for my TED talk

In society, there are certain foods that have been labelled as 'bad' and there are certain foods that have been labelled as 'good' and then somewhere along the way, we have given them a moral value. They've sort of become intrinsically linked to how good of a person we judge ourselves to be. It's pretty wild when you think about it.

Ever heard someone say "I'm being good" when avoiding a particular food group? *(That used to be me, one hundred percent, I was that person.)*

Essentially what this says is - If I eat a 'good' food, I am a good person or I am 'being good'

The same goes for 'bad' foods, I'm sure you've thought 'if I eat x y z I am being bad'

That seemingly throwaway statement actually holds a lot of power.

The label of guilt *(I am being 'bad')* leads us to feel shame and we then find ourselves thinking if I'm being 'bad', I am bad.

It's a toxic pattern of thinking that really keeps us stuck in a disordered mindset.

So, I really want you to hear me when I say this…

Food does not have the power to make anyone a good or a bad person.
Your worth is not determined by the food you consume.

Now if you're questioning what I'm saying or not onboard. That's perfectly understandable. One time of day I would have dismissed this line of thinking too. Labelling foods was ingrained in me. It was a big part of how I viewed myself. Changing my language and thoughts about food took practice, but breaking away from this way of thinking is essential for recovery so I've designed a bunch of prompts to help you unpack your own feelings around the matter.

Be sure to take your time as you navigate them.

Prompt: Make a list of foods you consider to be 'bad' and a list which you consider to be 'good'. It doesn't have to include every single thing ever, aim for five to ten of each, but feel free to add more if you wish.

Once you have an idea of the labels you hold, it's time to try and understand how they came to be.

Scan down the lists and address each item in turn.

Ask yourself: *Did you come up with the label for it? Did it come from someone you know? Or was it something society has pushed?*

The idea here is to start questioning why you've labelled it as such in the first place.

Now, I want you to write out your thoughts on the following:

Prompt: How would you feel if you ate one of the foods from your 'bad' list?

How would you feel if someone you care about ate one of the foods from your 'bad' list? Would you think the same things of them that you think of yourself?

How about one of the foods from the 'good' list, how would you feel if you ate one of those?

Prompt: What feeling do these labels give you? If you were to let go of all those labels, how would you feel?

Would letting go of those labels change your relationships with those foods?

Prompt: If I asked you to approach foods as neutral, how does that make you feel?

Next time you catch yourself attributing a label could you instead make the food neutral? Could you just make it a 'nothing' food?

Now if you're shaking your head thinking, but not all foods are equal, some are nutritionally better for you than others. I'm not discounting that. Though all foods have their place. What I'm trying to get at here in these prompts is the emphasis we put on the label and how that label impacts our feelings about ourselves if we consume that food.

If you've worked through these prompts and found them particularly challenging, that's completely understandable. I'm really proud of you for tackling them. I hope they help you to see that our language around food is powerful and it matters. Sending you a big hug and a high five for all your hard work.

Food & Eating Rules

For the final part of stage two, I want you to explore your feelings around any self-imposed food and eating rules *(just to be clear, an eating rule is based on how you consume food, i.e., not eating after a certain time and a food rule is based on avoiding certain foods.)*

When living with an eating disorder we tend to have a plethora of these rules and they become so entrenched in our life that it can be hard to recall where they even came from. In recovery, it's important that we start to dismantle them and see them for what they are, so let's give it a go.

Prompt: What are some eating rules you have and why?

I'm talking about the restrictive, negative kind. I think it's important to make that distinction because in recovery, an eating rule of committing to breakfast each day is a huge positive but, I prefer not to label it as a rule, instead I'd call it a commitment.

What I want you to think about here is any eating rules fuelled by limitations.

List out some which come to mind.

Prompt: Looking at the list you've made. Are there any which you have learnt to let go of so far? If so, how did that make you feel? Is there one you would like to let go of next?

Prompt: Where do you think these eating rules have come from? What beliefs underpin them?

A few examples of where these rules might have come from: *family, books, magazines, celebrity 'what I eat in a day' articles, social media, something in the news, something at school.*

Prompt: If you had to list out the food rules that you are still holding onto, what are they? How would stepping away from them make you feel?

Prompt: Are there certain foods you feel guilty for eating? Are there certain foods you are still avoiding?

Have you attempted to eat them? If not, why not. What stops you?

What would eating that food mean to you? How would you feel?

Prompt: If you fear eating, why do you think you fear eating certain foods? If you don't feel like you fear food, what feelings do you associate with food? What do you believe food has the power to do?

Prompt: Have the feelings that you associate with food changed since stage one?

Prompt: Looking at all the food and eating rules you've listed out; would you suggest for someone else to follow them? If not, why not?

Prompt: If you could let go of one rule tomorrow, what would it be? Can you make that happen over the coming week?

* * *

Take a deep breath in through the nose, hold for four, breathe out through the mouth.

That my lovely friends, is the end of stage two.

Can you hear that?

That's me cheering really loud right now! You've done it! You've worked through all of the reflections for stage two!

I know there was a lot to unpack and work through, but you did it, you persisted.

Feel free to have a look at the table below and if you feel you are ready to move onto stage three, go right ahead. If you want some time to sit with and process everything you've worked through, I suggest keeping up or reintroducing your *Daily* journal entries until you feel it's time for stage three. As always, remember this is *your* recovery and you set the pace. I'm proud of you.

Throughout Stage 1	Ready to move to Stage 2 when...	Throughout Stage 2	Ready to move to Stage 3 when...	By the end of Stage 3
Fighting the constant urge to binge, purge, restrict.	You might still have urges, but you are no longer acting upon them each time.	You're eating more freely but still dealing with the mental aspects around food. Urges lessening.	Challenging and overcoming the mental aspects of food and eating behaviours. Urges lessening.	Maintaining positive physical habits and not engaging in any harmful behaviours. Urges ceased.
Fear of eating & food measurements (calories, macros etc.)	Managing to eat more regular meals, not feeling as controlled by food measurements	No longer feeling out of control around food, significant trust regained. Not feeling the need to measure foods.	Still not feeling out of control around food, trust remains. Not feeling the need to measure foods.	Eating freely. Food sits in proper perspective in your life and does not dominate it.
Frequent moods swings & heightened emotions.	Moods growing more stable, though still a lot of emotional ups and downs.	Feeling more emotionally stable. Maintaining healthy relationships with those around you.	Generally, feel good but still like you're searching for the last piece of the puzzle but you're not sure what it is (cryptic I know).	Feeling positive about the future, strong and stable in your recovery.
Fighting the urge to over exercise.	Exercise might still feel problematic.	Challenging your relationship with moving your body.	Learning to move your body from a place of love and not fear or punishment.	Moving your body from a place of love.
Constant bodychecking. (Only if this is a feature for you)	Bodychecking lessening.	Bodychecking ideally ceased.	Growing acceptance of your body.	Accepting and appreciative of your body.

13

STAGE THREE

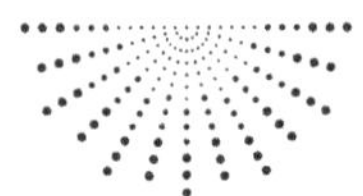

CHALLENGING THOUGHTS

"When you throw away the idea of perfection, you make a lot more space for joy." – Yung Pueblo.

Prerequisite: Completion of stages one & two

Your goal: To stop negative thoughts in their tracks and reduce the ones that take hold.

Oh, my goodness I am so proud of you! *(I know I always say that but that's because it's true.)* I know you've been working so hard at this, and I am so pleased you're feeling ready to start the final stage. There is no doubt in my mind that you are feeling much stronger by now. Both physically and mentally. And if you're reading this and doubting just how far you've come. Think back to stage one. Take a look at some of your journal entries. That's huge progress. You've come SO far!

By now, your foundational habits and journal practice is probably pretty solid. You're probably feeling much better emotionally on the whole too but might still be battling that inner critic. Thing is, after years of negative thought patterns, it's hard to make them just stop. It takes practice. And that is what this stage is all about.

Remember that diagram from the very beginning? The one where we work backwards? Well, I'm pleased to report, that you are now at the start. You've addressed the actions' part and unpacked a lot of your beliefs too, but there's still a little way more to go. It's time to dive into them a bit further and learn to nip those negative thoughts in the bud too! We have to tackle all three aspects for a successful recovery, and I'm pleased to report that you're nearly there!

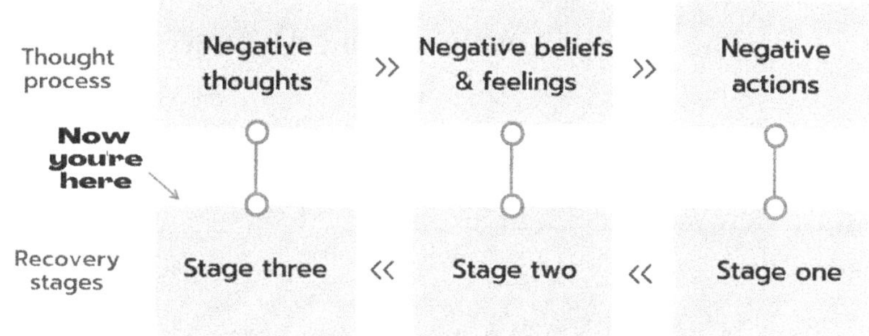

How you're going to get there…

You're going to reflect and then reflect some more!

Stage three is where you learn how to stop your negative thoughts in their tracks and get that inner critic to shush once and for all. Not only that but I want you to take an objective look at your eating disorder. I want you to dig deep. This is where you set yourself up for long-term success. You learn to set boundaries and re-write any negative beliefs that might be lingering.

What is the suggested timeframe for this stage?

As with stage two, you can do a prompt every day or pick an area to focus on each week.

For example: You could set yourself the goal of completing all the prompts in the diet culture section in a week, or you could do a prompt from that section each day.

As there are only four prompts in that section it means you could move through the material quicker if you completed one each day. However, deep reflection is the key so be mindful to go at a pace which allows for that. And remember, there is no right and wrong. You set the pace. This is *your* recovery.

The Recover You Journaling Method.

Important, don't skip this one

Time for a new stage and a more simplified version of the RYJM for the last one.

Since this section is all about challenging thoughts, I've decided to simplify the format and just focus on the *Reflections* section. If you want to keep up with your *Space to Cope* and *Daily* entries from the previous stages, please feel free to. This is your journaling practice, so always do what feels right for you.

14

REFLECTIONS

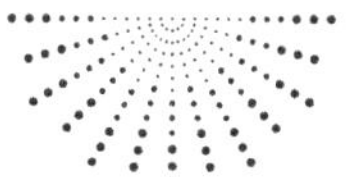

Let's get straight into it...

Self-worth

I know we've spoken about self-esteem, self-confidence, and even self-validation... so you might be thinking, another self-thing? Why? What's the difference?

Well, the short answer is that they're all similar, all linked, they just show up a little differently in our hearts and minds.

Self-worth is how we view our worth and value as a human being.

It's what they call a core belief which means it's pretty stable over-time and doesn't tend to change day to day, which is great if our self-worth is positive, however that's not always the case.

When we come into the world, we're born not questioning our worth. As such we're not even aware of its existence. We simply are as we are and show up in the world exactly as that. Our worth comes solely from within and it's a really beautiful thing.

But, as we grow through life, our self-worth can often take a battering. The people, environment and situations we encounter start to shape how we view our worth. It becomes entangled with all of these external factors, and we start to put conditions on it.

I must add, that's not the case for everyone but in my experience, people with eating disorders have a tendency to put a lot of these conditions on themselves. Now often we're not aware of the conditions, they just sort of happen.

So that's our job here, to explore our self-worth and see if it was a bit of a driver in some of our ed behaviours.

Let's start unpacking…

Prompt: Right now, in this very moment, where does your worth come from?

It might be something you've never thought much about. If the question doesn't strike a chord with you, instead ask yourself, *what makes you feel worthy? What makes you feel valued?*

Pause here and write your entry, then come back and read the next paragraph.

* * *

You're back! Hi!

Okay, so similarly, to confidence and validation, a lot of sources of our worth and how valued we feel can be external. When asked, people typically reel off things such as their job or job title, their financial situation, their physical attributes or other peoples' opinions of them. If they're active on social media, this can be a prime source of external validation too, the more likes and interactions on a post, the more 'worthy' and 'valued' they feel.

If you'd have asked me in this stage, I would have still been battling the belief that I was only valuable if I was useful to others and looked a certain way.

Thing is, all these external conditions give away your power. You're like a hamster continually running in a wheel, chasing… well who knows what. The point is, it's ever-changing dependent on whichever external condition you measure it by and you're not in control of that. But the good news is you can be.

You can take back your power. You can stop letting external conditions dictate your worth to you. You can say *'hey, I am enough as I am, and my worth is not conditional.'* Sure, all those other things can be bonuses on top of your already established awesomeness, but they are not the sole determinants. You and your mindset are.

I know right, easier said than done, but it can be done.

The aim of this section is to dig a little deeper and get to know where your self-worth is coming from. Then *(if needed)* in the following sections we will work on restoring it.

Suggested affirmation: I know that in this moment, I am enough, and my worth does not have conditions attached.

Prompt: Do you feel worthy of love? Is it conditional?

I'm going to get real with you here. This prompt made me feel so uncomfortable. I found myself answering it as I wrote it and still putting conditions on my own worth *(face palm!)*

Well, someone would only love me if I was kind, generous and doing things for that person too. They couldn't just love me for me, regardless, that's a selfish request... I must be of use to them...

Now don't get me wrong, your worth can shine through in acts of kindness and compassion for others, but it doesn't determine it. We are all worthy as we are *(I'm saying this as much for myself as I am for you!)*

Suggested affirmation: My worth and being here is not conditional.

Prompt: Do you feel valued? Is it conditional?

Suggested affirmation: I value myself and all that I am.

Prompt: Do you feel deserving of good things? Is it conditional?

Suggested affirmation: I deserve good things.

Prompt: Do you treat yourself with respect? Do you feel deserving of respect?

Suggested affirmation: I treat myself with respect and honour all that I am.

Prompt: Do you view yourself as a good person? What does being a good person mean to you?

Suggested affirmation: My worth shines through in my kindness, compassion, empathy and respect for others.

Prompt: What are three things you love about yourself? If you read this and cringe, firstly ask yourself why? And then re-frame, instead write out three skills you have which you are proud of.

Suggested affirmation: I am proud of the person I am.

Letting go of the need to be perfect

If you completed the previous section and found that your self-worth is a little low, letting go of the need to be perfect can help in restoring it.

The need to be perfect often plays a big role in eating disorders. Letting go of it takes practice and time. Since this is stage three, I'm thinking you have *(for the most part)* stepped away from that way of thinking in terms of your eating, however it can rear its head in other areas of our life *(such as self-worth).*

If any of this resonates with you, I want you to take a moment *(or rather several moments)* to reflect on the prompts below. If you're not sure, have a scan through the prompts and if they don't strike a chord with you, feel free to skip ahead to the next section.

Prompt: Do you feel a need to be 'perfect'? What areas of your life does that show up in for you?

For example: I no longer feel a need to be perfect in my eating however, I do in my working life.

Suggested affirmation: I release the need to be perfect. It simply doesn't exist.

Prompt: What does it mean to be 'perfect'?

Suggested affirmation: Perfect doesn't exist. I am enough as I am.

Prompt: What does being 'perfect' give you? Do you associate it with reward? Does striving for it alleviate a feeling in you?

Suggested affirmation: I strive for meaning in all that I do, not perfection.

Prompt: How does being viewed as 'perfect' make you feel? What feeling are you hoping to achieve by being 'perfect'?

Suggested affirmation: I am enough, I have enough, and I do enough.

Prompt: How do you view your perceived 'imperfections'?

Suggested affirmation: Through mistakes I learn, and I grow.

Prompt: How do you view those same 'imperfections' in others?

Suggested affirmation: Mistakes are part of being human.

Prompt: If you feel you are still chasing 'perfection', what does your quest for it stop you doing in life?

Suggested affirmation: Today I will focus on what is possible.

Prompt: Are there things you would try if you didn't hold yourself to such standards?

Suggested affirmation: I release any unrealistic and unreasonable standards.

Prompt: Where do you think these standards come from? Would you expect someone else to live by the same standards?

Suggested affirmation: I free myself from unrealistic standards.

Good on you for working through this section. Although it doesn't seem like a really heavy subject, it can be uncomfortable to address the role of 'perfect' in our lives. I hope you found it beneficial, and it ties in nicely to our next topic as often I find in striving for 'perfection' we use self-talk to berate ourselves.

Let's get into it…

Self-talk & your thoughts

Prompt: What are the most common thoughts you have about yourself?

I want you to list out whatever comes to mind.

For example: I talk too much, why am I so clumsy? At least I'm talkative, I can strike up a conversation with anyone, I wish my hair was thicker.

(Ps - This is the nice PG version, my inner critic used to be vicious, truly awful... so if yours is too, I hear you, put it all down here.)

Once you've done that, come back to this spot and we'll continue.

Looking at your list, I want you to work through the following...

Prompt: Are the thoughts mostly positive or negative? What aspect of you are they related to? How does this inner dialogue make you feel?

I'm going to take a wild guess and say that a lot of them are probably a bit negative, some even darn right mean. And maybe they're related to a range of things from our interaction with others, our bodies, our intelligence, maybe our performance. Whatever area it is, on the whole we don't tend to be very nice to ourselves, but don't you worry, I've got a prompt and a couple of tasks that are going to help you work through this and shut down that noise once and for all.

First up, the prompt. Now remember way back in stage one when you wrote a breakup letter to your ed? *(The one where you took a stance and told it you were sick of its shit!)*

Well, this is similar to that, but instead I want you to focus on your inner dialogue, or rather the inner dialogue that your ed has perpetuated.

Prompt: Use this space in your journal to stand up to the negative voice and break up with it once and for all.

This is your space to vent all your frustrations, to get angry with it and tell it to leave.

For example:

Dear misery maker! I'm done with you. I'm sick of listening to your negativity. Nothing you say is true. You manifested as part of my eating disorder, and you are not who I am at my core. I'm done. I want you to leave. I'm ready to live my life to the fullest. I deserve to live my life with freedom.

If this doesn't resonate with you, instead ask yourself: *How would I feel if this dialogue didn't run through my head constantly? What would it free me up to think about instead? How would my life change for the better?*

For example:

Right now, my mind never feels free and honestly, I'm sick of feeling this way. If I imagine my life without the negative voice, I feel so much lighter in my soul, I feel confident and free to be me.

Next, it's time to take action…

Task: Over the next few days, I want you to keep a list in your phone or here in your notebook. Phone is typically easier as you can do it in the moment. Every time a negative thought comes up, I want you to keep a note of it. Try to separate yourself from the thought, don't spend too much time dwelling on it. Just note it down. At the end of the few days, I want you to come back here with the list *(for reference, I did this task myself over two days.)*

Do you have your list?

Right, now I want you to give it a read, *how do you feel?*

When I carried out this task, I was truly shocked. I knew my thoughts could be mean but noting them down made me a little horrified at just how harsh they were. I laughed at some things but that's because they were so ridiculous. It was a wake-up call.

Good news is, there are a couple of tried and tested ways of combating them.

Time to break free!

Now, there are two options… you can use one or both. I opted for both since I figured that would have the greatest impact.

The first option:

I want you to think of yourself as a little kid. Cast your mind back to that version of yourself. The one that just showed up in the world as they were, so sweet and full of love.

Now look at your list and imagine saying whatever negative thoughts are on it to that childlike version of yourself. I'm betting you can't. I tried, I felt too sad. Little Soph didn't deserve that hate, so neither does the adult version! And the same goes for you!

I invite you to give it a try. Next time you catch a negative thought bubbling up *(and it does take practice)* pause, remember the child-like you and ask if you would say it to them. No, you would not. Job done.

. . .

The second option:

Call yourself out on anything nasty you say to yourself. Yup. As soon as a negative thought creeps on in you have to shut that shit down. Firmly say no, I am not doing this today. I often find it helps to say it out loud. And then you move on with your day.

I realise it sounds almost a bit too simple, but it is truly life-changing! Once you get into the swing of it, it becomes second nature and after practicing it for most of last year, I can honestly say I don't find nearly as many thoughts even cropping up. They know they don't get airtime from me anymore!

Now I can't take credit for these methods at all, they're not my creation but instead borrowed from a really great book called Body Talk by Katie Sturino, which I highly recommend reading at this stage in your recovery. Not only is Katie hilarious, but a beacon of light in celebrating and accepting oneself. A perfect stage three read!

I hope these techniques help you as much as they have me. Before we move onto the next topic, I just wanted to talk a little more on thoughts…

Your thoughts matter. Like, really matter. But…
Not everything you think is true.

Cue brain explode emoji! *(Jokes)*

I'm going to explain what I mean here because it might seem a bit confusing…

Say you have a negative thought about yourself *(which quickly sparks a train of them)* such as *'I look terrible in this top, my skins terrible, why is my hair so dry, why do I never look put together.'*

When you give these thoughts attention; they take hold and start changing your mood. *'I feel gross. Why do I never look good? I feel like shit.'* Now you don't really want to see anyone or leave the house.

Thing is, once that thought *(or series of thoughts)* have been given attention, your brain then looks for real world information to confirm what you've told it. How crazy is that! Before you know it, you'll start seeing brittle hair loss ad's everywhere, everyone will seem to have way better hair than you, you'll catch your hair reflection in every mirror… you get the idea.

Now, have you ever bought something thinking, I've never seen that before? And then suddenly you start seeing the same thing everywhere. It's called the Frequency Illusion. Our brains form a cognitive bias and then after noticing something for the first time, start to notice it everywhere, leading you to believe that it occurs way more often than it does.

So, I'm sure you can see where I'm going with this…

If you spend your days thinking and speaking negative shit to yourself, your brain will keep on searching for evidence to confirm it and guess what, it will find a whole heap of it. Even though these thoughts are just that, thoughts. Not facts. They're fleeting moments of consciousness that we can either choose to ignore… or pay attention to.

Like I said…

Your thoughts matter.
Are they always true? F*ck no!
But what you give attention to matters.

Self-compassion

Let's move onto another self-thing. This time it's self-compassion. Stage three really is the stage of 'the self' and for good reason. Getting to know ourselves, acknowledging and accepting all parts of ourselves is one of the greatest things we can do, especially in recovery.

We've talked about letting go of the need to be perfect and improving our self-talk, and one of the ways we can do this is through self-compassion.

First up, I want you to explore where you're at.

Prompt: Which areas of your life are you the most self-critical? How could you show yourself more kindness and understanding in these?

Suggested affirmation: I am worthy of care and understanding, no matter what.

Prompt: In what ways *do* you show yourself kindness? In what ways *could* you show yourself kindness?

Suggested affirmation: I commit to being kind to myself in all that I do.

Prompt: Do you make the same allowances for yourself as you do for others? or do you have different standards that only you must meet?

Suggested affirmation: I treat myself the way I would treat my closest friend.

Prompt: Do you think others deserve more compassion than you? What makes someone deserving of compassion in your eyes?

Suggested affirmation: When I show myself compassion, I am able to show others more compassion too.

Prompt: Do you feel worthy of compassion?

Suggested affirmation: I am worthy of kindness and compassion.

Prompt: Think of a recent situation where you've been hard on yourself. What would you say to someone else dealing with the same situation? What words of encouragement would you give them?

Suggested affirmation: Today, I speak words of kindness to myself and others.

I want you to take a moment to review your answers in this section so far.

If I now asked you, *are you compassionate towards yourself? What would you say?*

Moving forward, it's something we have to make a commitment to because it has such a huge flow on effect to all the other areas of our life. If we show ourselves compassion it boosts our mood, it helps to reduce stress, it helps with our self-worth, body image and motivation. And they are all things we need for a solid recovery.

So, I invite you to answer the prompt below…

Prompt: What more can you do to show yourself compassion today and moving forward?

Ask yourself: How can I respond to myself with more compassion? What are some acts that would show myself kindness?

Here are a few of my favourite ways:

Change how you view mistakes instead see them as learning opportunities.

Don't negatively label yourself (or others) – 'I'm so stupid' or 'I'm so clumsy' etc.

Accept your emotions without casting harsh judgments of yourself.

Practice acts of self-care such as getting enough sleep and taking time out for you.

Set boundaries which prioritise your own well-being.

Suggested affirmation: I am learning to cherish my unique self and all that I am.

Prompt: Identify one area of your recovery that you are struggling with right now. How can you bring more self-compassion to this situation? What would it feel like to approach yourself with kindness and understanding?

What is an action you can take this week to implement that?

I'll share my own example from this stage here:

I am struggling to feel at peace with myself as I feel like I should be further along in my recovery. I feel so frustrated and angry with myself. When I feel like this, my negative self-talk starts up. I don't know how to bring more self-compassion to this situation. What could I do? I guess I could remind myself that everyone's journey looks different and that I can't be 'behind' in my own life. I think it would feel hard initially, but it would be really nice to give myself a break.

My action is to write myself a pep talk and stick it on the back of my bedroom door.

Suggested affirmation: I am learning to give myself grace in my recovery journey.

Ready for the next section?

Let's move on…

Body Talk & Beliefs

In this section I'm going to ask you to delve into your past. This can be a particularly painful section to work through as a lot of feelings might re-surface, but I want you to know that it can be a particularly cathartic section too. At the end of this section, you'll have an understanding of where some of your attitudes and beliefs around bodies and food developed. This section also provides an opportunity to respond to any hurtful comments and events you might have experienced in the past. It's a chance to stand up for yourself here on the pages and have your voice heard. Make sure to take the time you need as you work through the prompts here. I'm sending you a big old hug and a high five for tackling this.

Prompt: Growing up, how were bodies spoken about in your house? Was someone's physical appearance often commented on? Was your own physical appearance commented on? If so, how did that make you feel?

Prompt: Growing up, were there certain attitudes or rules around food and eating in your house? If so, how did they make you feel?

Prompt: How did your parents *(or caregivers)* talk about their own bodies growing up?

Prompt: Was dieting discussed in your house growing up? How about shaming someone for their size? Or judging someone for the type of food they consume?

Looking back over your answers in this section so far, how does that make you feel today as an adult, would you say the same things to a child? If you would, which parts would you say? If not, why not?

I just want to add, this isn't a blame game, it's simply an opportunity to think about the environment where your attitudes around bodies were formed and work on that narrative moving forward.

Prompt: Growing up, what beliefs did you hold about your body? Did you have a desire to change your body?

Prompt: Growing up, is there a particular stand out event which made you want to change your body or a particular event that made you overly aware of your body?

I realise this might be a really hard prompt to work through so if you find yourself shaking your head, thinking you can't tackle it. That's completely fine. You don't have to. You're in charge here.

For those that want to give it a go, I want you to use this space to stand up for yourself.

Say the things you wish you'd said in that situation.

Truthfully, I have so many examples for this one, I could write a book. I chose to share one that made me really angry for a long time, but I've since managed to work through it thanks to my journaling practice.

My event: I was about ten years old, and I hadn't seen my grandma for several months. When she visited one summer, I ran into the room all excited to say hi to her, I was eating a packet of my favourite crisps, loving life.

Instead of greeting me with a hug (or even a smile!) She instead turned and looked at me in disgust and said to my mum 'gosh hasn't she put on a lot of weight, should she really be eating that.'

It might not seem like much, but this comment changed how I saw food. It made me aware that my body was different, and it made me feel so ashamed of myself and my eating.

Now, this is the part where I get to stand up for myself.

My response today:

This is what I've longed to say. I realise that you're saying this because you place all of your value in your appearance. I realise this is something that was common in your generation and therefore it seems second nature to you. However, your words to me are rude, uncalled for and judgmental. I ask that you don't comment on my appearance or what food I consume anymore.

Thank you.

In my head I imagine speaking up for myself in that moment, I smile and walk away with my head held high. I feel satisfied and at peace that I've finally had my voice heard.

I invite you to do the same.

Body Acceptance

I'm going to get real with you now…

To overcome the illness, the compulsive behaviours and the obsession of my eating disorder, I had to let go of all food rules. This meant adopting intentional intuitive eating initially and then moving to full on intuitive eating once I had recovered a little more. Here I re-learned to recognise my hunger, eating all foods without restriction and subsequently I did gain weight. You might have experienced something similar.

Now, initially this was really hard to accept. My body had changed, and I felt disconnected from it. I really struggled with what to wear. I worried what people would think. And I didn't know what to do to change my feelings towards it.

Remember how I spoke about societies limited definition of health in stage two? Where the sole emphasis is on your physical body? Now remember where I said viewing my health more holistically had helped me in my recovery? Well, this is one of the times where that came in.

Upon reflection I saw that I now treated my body with care. I also respected myself and my recovery. I felt mentally strong, emotionally in check. Was I really about to reduce all of that progress to a single marker on a scale? *(For the billionth time in my life)*

F*ck no.

And guess what, bodies change. Shocking I know!

Despite what the media pushes. Despite what they try to sell you to change that.

Bodies change. And your body will change throughout your life.

And that's okay. Better than okay in fact. It means you're here, living life and experiencing all that it is to be human. And that doesn't have to look a certain way. We're all unique.

But more than anything here, I want you to know and remember that you are so much more than a body.

If this body acceptance struggle resonates with you in any way, I invite you to explore the next few prompts, so you can start finding ways to make peace with your body asap, if not, skip these and make your way onto the next section.

Prompt: How are you feeling about your body? If you've experienced changes, how are you feeling about them?

If you're feeling negatively towards your body, I want you to think of your recovery and your health today, holistically. Take into account your mental and spiritual wellbeing, your social connections and activities, even the environment around you.

Then list out some wins which you've had in those areas since you started out in your recovery.

Prompt: Do your body changes influence how you think, feel or value yourself? If so, why?

Prompt: How do you want to feel about your body? Are there steps you could take to make peace with your body without trying to change it? What is keeping you from appreciating your body as it is right now?

Just a word on this one, your aim doesn't have to be to feel super positive towards your body, it can be to just feel more neutral towards it and accepting.

Prompt: What are you grateful to your body for?

Prompt: Right now, in this moment, do you feel connected to your body?

It's really common to reach this stage of recovery and feel an element of disconnection from your body given the changes it's been through.

If you do, here are a few of my favourite ways to start getting that connection back:

Stretching and yoga

Soothing baths and slathering yourself in moisturiser after

Singing and dancing, not typically at the same time, but on occasion

Resting when needed and thanking your body for all that it does *(I affirm this out loud)*

If none of the above resonate with you, what's something instead you could do to show your body some appreciation?

Prompt: What does taking care of your body look like to you? What are three things you can do this week to care for your body?

Prompt: Thinking ahead to the future, what will taking care of your body help you to achieve?

Moving your body

Body acceptance and the movement we choose for our bodies go hand in hand. Even at this stage of recovery it can be hard to know what type of intentional movement to engage in since many of us have battled with overexercising in the past.

Now, I realise this doesn't speak to everyone. Some of you might have sunk into a fantastic new routine where you listen entirely to your body or for some of you your relationship with moving your body might never have been a part of your disorder. If either of these describe you, I suggest skipping ahead to the next section.

However, if you're struggling to incorporate some sort of movement into your life and very much want to, but are still getting panicked by old habits or feelings of I 'should' return to the gym, then this section is for you.

As a once chronic over exerciser, I fell into the latter group. I battled with moving my body throughout my entire recovery. I'd get surges of "I should go back to the gym" or "I'm not doing enough; I should start up a new routine," which *(always and inevitably)* involved me working out at least five days a week.

It's only now that I've made peace with it and don't let the old feelings creep *in (or if they do I tell them to clear off)* and all the questions I worked through to get there, I've incorporated into the prompts below.

I invite you to explore and reflect where you're at and by the end of this section, you'll have more of an idea why you're moving your body, how to overcome issues around it and the role it can play in your life moving forward.

Prompt: How is your current relationship with moving your body? Do you currently engage in any intentional movement for your body?

For reference, this can be anything from a walk right through to lifting weights.

If so, why have you chosen to move your body in this particular way? How does moving your body in this way make you feel?

If not, is there some form of movement that you would like to incorporate back into your life? Why would you like to do this type of movement in particular?

Is there a type of movement or workout you think you 'should' be doing? If so, why do you think you 'should' be doing it?

Task: For those of you that have tried incorporating movement back into your life but have found yourself struggling, I want you to try and break down the scenarios where that has happened.

For example: I tried going to a few strength based group classes that I used to enjoy but found myself physically struggling because I hadn't done that type of movement for so long. I looked around the room comparing myself to others, berating my efforts. I left feeling defeated, deflated, and downright miserable.

After you've written out your scenario, I want you to ask yourself: *What does this tell me?*

What my scenario told me:

- *Group classes bring out comparison in me and spark my harsh inner critic.*
- *Doing the same workouts I used to do peak eating disorder make me feel bad.*

What I then want you to ask yourself: *What is the goal of doing this type of movement?*

You can either write it down or simply just contemplate your answer. I personally like to write it out because it helps me think about it that bit clearer.

My answer: Well, I used to enjoy this class (kind of) it made me feel good because I really pushed myself and I was really good at it. My goal was... to push myself.

I then want you to ask yourself: *Is that still something I want to do now?*

If so, why? What is your belief about this type of movement? Do you feel a sense of identity tied to it?

If not, what is your goal for moving your body?

My answer: I don't want to push myself, but I do feel like those classes formed part of my identity. At the back of my mind, I think I told myself I'd always go back once I got better. However, I really just wanted to get moving again and improve my flexibility and strength because my back's sore from all the desk work I do!

Finally, I want you to ask: *Could I do this with a different type of movement?*

My answer: Yes. I could follow a plethora of videos at home, or I could try a really gentle in-person yoga class. If I seek out a group class, it needs to be gentle so I don't feel the need to compare.

For those of you currently undertaking some sort of movement, I want you to check in and ask yourself:

Prompt: How are my thoughts during and after moving my body? Are any old thought patterns creeping in? If they are, am I managing to shake them off or do they linger?

Do my choices of movement feel joyful or obligatory?

Am I resting when my body asks me to?

Are my expectations and routine rational? Do they sit in proper perspective in my life?

Lastly, a question for everyone:

Is there a type of movement you'd like to try?

Anything from hiking, swimming through to old-timey dancing. If there is anything that comes to mind, follow that pull. If you once were a chronic over exerciser, it can be nice to do some things that re-connect your body with movement without placing conditions on it.

If you feel any resistance to this question, I want you to write out why.

For example: If you are scared to try something new or scared that old patterns will re-emerge, write that down. It could simply be that you don't want to incorporate anything new into your life right now.

Every prompt is an opportunity to learn that bit more about ourselves, even if the answer isn't what we think it will be.

Moving forward, whatever methods you choose *(or don't, no shade here)* I want you to always ensure you approach it from a place of love, care and appreciation for your body. If you find yourself saying I 'should' do this, it always pays to question, *why?*

Diet culture

I realise this might be an uncomfortable topic, but it wouldn't feel right to not address it.

Despite committing to our recovery, there's no denying that the screams of diet culture can be really loud. We are constantly barraged with diet propaganda and the latest miracle 'cures' to any 'problem' with our body we might have. From internet ads and magazine covers through to conversations in the break room at work. It can be exhausting, especially when you've worked so hard to recover.

First, I want you to check in with where you are at on this one because it is pervasive in our society therefore, we need to first acknowledge our feelings around it and then make a plan to tackle it so we can remain strong in our recovery.

Prompt: Are you feeling pressures of diet culture? If so, has anything in particular sparked those feelings?

Is there a particular area of your life or an environment where you encounter a lot of diet culture chatter?

Prompt: What are your go-to coping skills for dealing with any recovery wobbles you may encounter as a result of this?

A few of mine are to read other people's recovery stories, read books on body acceptance, positivity and/or neutrality and to read my own journal entries from stage one and remember how far I've come.

Prompt: Are you currently using social media? If so, do you feel you've curated a space which supports your recovery as best as it possibly can?

Prompt: Overall, are you still feeling supported in your recovery?

The reason I ask is that at this stage of recovery, people around us can almost forget that we are still recovering. Social support and community are both so important for recovery longevity, so, if you do find yourself feeling the need, do reach out to a local or online recovery support group. Connecting with others who understand what you're experiencing is a game changer and can really help to overcome diet culture wobbles.

Now, before we move onto our next topic, I have five things that I want you to remember if ever you start feeling the pull of diet culture BS…

1. Everything is designed to sell you something.
2. You have to be selective of who you listen to.
3. You have to be selective of what media you consume.
4. You don't need to change your body to be accepted and loved.
5. That acceptance and love, starts with you.

Cue, mic drop.

And just like that, it's time for the last set of prompts.

The Ultimate Reflection

Apologies for the dramatic title but it really does sum it up. In this final set of prompts I'm going to ask you to take an objective look back on your eating disorder and how it came to be. In doing so I want you to try and set any judgements of yourself aside and see it as best as you can from a sort of neutral perspective. The idea behind this, is so that you can further understand yourself and put into perspective the role your ed played in your life.

Before you take a look back and start to put pen to paper, I just want to remind you one last time to go gentle with yourself. Take as much time as you need here and remember, nobody consciously chooses to have an eating disorder. I say that because these prompts might trigger some of those types of thoughts, so I want to be very clear. None of this has been your fault, you are not to blame. None of us chose this, but we did choose recovery and that is one of the bravest most important choices you'll ever make for yourself and for those you love.

Hear me when I say, I am SO proud of you.

Okay, time for some slow deep breaths to get us in the right mindset.

Breathe in for three through the nose and let it out slowly through the mouth. Repeat that at least three times.

Now it's journal time.

Prompt: Looking back over the course of your life so far, when do you think your eating disorder started?

Prompt: Did you have 'goals' related to your ed? If so, what did you think they would bring you? Why did you think they would bring you that? If not, feel free to skip this prompt.

For example: I had weight related goals and I thought they would solve all of my problems if I achieved them. I placed all my value in this one metric. It seemed like something I could control. Growing up, so much value was placed on this in my world that I thought it was all that mattered.

Prompt: Upon reflection, do you now think you used your ed to cope?

Prompt: Do you think you used your ed to feel in control? If so, do you feel in control of your life now in a different way?

Prompt: What did your ed bring to your life? What did it take?

Prompt: Do you feel at peace with food today? How would you describe your relationship with it?

Prompt: Why do you think you might have developed an ed? What contributed? Upon reflection, is there something you now recognise which drove you to it? A tipping point?

For example: Through my journaling I realised that I was constantly seeking ways to be validated by others. My self-worth was tied deeply to my body and appearance. The emphasis I placed on these took hold as a child and continued throughout my life. My tipping point was an extremely stressful period of my life.

Prompt: Do you recall or feel like a particular event triggered your ed?

Please don't feel you have to write about it here if it's too painful. I know this can be a really heavy prompt. Instead, you can choose to write about all the emotions you felt during that period of your life when your eating disorder took hold.

For example: I felt angry, really angry but I felt like I had no voice. No way of expressing it. No one to express it to. I'd kept everything held in for so long I sort of burst. I felt so many things. Like I was spiralling out of control. Like I was in control. It was a roller-coaster that changed on the daily.

Take a deep breath in and out after that one.

Feel free to put your hand on your heart and let yourself know: *you are safe, you are loved and today is different.* This can be a nice one to repeat to yourself in times of anxiety and overwhelm.

I am sending you the biggest hug right now. I'm so sorry for whatever it is you've had to go through.

Looking forward, it can be a good idea to go through the emotions you've expressed in the previous set of prompts and make sure that you have a plan on how to cope with that emotion in the future.

For example:

Anger: When I am angry, in the moment I will pause, close my eyes and take a few deep breaths. I will focus on calming myself. I will not hold in what I want to express. Moving forward, I commit to communicating my feelings, even if it's not directly with the person concerned. I will not keep things bottled up anymore and I will make sure I speak to people about what's going on with me.

After the intensity of this section, I want to finish on a high so let's switch gears and celebrate all the things recovery has brought to your life so far.

Prompt: What does recovery mean to you today?

Remember way back in stage one when I asked you to think of your definition? Well, how do the two compare? I hope you're feeling better than you could have ever imagined.

Prompt: List five amazing things choosing recovery has brought to your life.

More if you like! Celebrate all the wins, big and small.

* * *

How are you feeling?

You best be high fiving yourself right now!

I'm so happy that you're here reading this. That means you've put in the hours; you've put in the work, and you've journaled your way to a better place, mentally, physically, and emotionally *(either that or you've just skipped ahead and are reading this and if that is the case, scoot! Get back to the prompts!)*

In all seriousness, I'm writing this in awe of the person reading this, I'm so proud of you and I'm so glad you decided to give journaling a try. Thank you for being so open and making the Recover You Journaling Method part of your recovery journey.

If you're wondering how to incorporate journaling into your life moving forward, you can do what I do and check in with yourself on the pages each day. I don't use prompts; I just write out my waking thoughts and feelings, but it seems to get the job done. However, if you do prefer prompts, head on over to the Recover You website and sign up for the newsletter, where I throw in some bonus prompts from time to time or alternatively come find me on Instagram @letsrecoveryou where I share my latest thoughts on all things recovery.

Before I sign off, I just have a little ask and that is, if you found this guide to be helpful, please do leave a review and if you have any suggestions, improvements, or topics you'd like to see included, please do reach out to me and let me know. I created Recover You and wrote this guide for you and your input not only helps me to learn and grow but it helps others in their recovery too.

Thank you again for including me in your recovery.

And know that I'm always cheering you on.

Your friend with a pen!

Sophie B xx

Ps - If by the end of stage three, you're not feeling the things listed in the table that follows, please don't lose hope. The table is only a guide, and everyone has their own timeline.

What can be helpful in this scenario is to look back over your journal entries for the appropriate sections that you're struggling with. Here, you can look for any clues or commonalities that might have cropped up on the pages. Once you have an idea of them, you could 'free' journal about those topics (meaning you just write without prompts) and see if anything more comes through.

Additionally, you could use the information from your journal entries to seek out more guidance in that area, be it from a health-care professional or self-led through books and blogs.

Throughout Stage 1	Ready to move to Stage 2 when...	Throughout Stage 2	Ready to move to Stage 3 when...	By the end of Stage 3
Fighting the constant urge to binge, purge, restrict.	You might still have urges, but you are no longer acting upon them each time.	You're eating more freely but still dealing with the mental aspects around food. Urges lessening.	Challenging and overcoming the mental aspects of food and eating behaviours. Urges lessening.	Maintaining positive physical habits and not engaging in any harmful behaviours. Urges ceased.
Fear of eating & food measurements (calories, macros etc.)	Managing to eat more regular meals, not feeling as controlled by food measurements.	No longer feeling out of control around food, significant trust regained. Not feeling the need to measure foods.	Still not feeling out of control around food, trust remains. Not feeling the need to measure foods.	Eating freely. Food sits in proper perspective in your life and does not dominate it.
Frequent moods swings & heightened emotions.	Moods growing more stable, though still a lot of emotional ups and downs.	Feeling more emotionally stable. Maintaining healthy relationships with those around you.	Generally, feel good but still like you're searching for the last piece of the puzzle but you're not sure what it is (cryptic I know).	Feeling positive about the future, strong and stable in your recovery.
Fighting the urge to over exercise.	Exercise might still feel problematic.	Challenging your relationship with moving your body.	Learning to move your body from a place of love and not fear or punishment.	Moving your body from a place of love.
Constant bodychecking. (Only if this is a feature for you)	Bodychecking lessening.	Bodychecking ideally ceased.	Growing acceptance of your body.	Accepting and appreciative of your body.

15
MOVING FORWARD

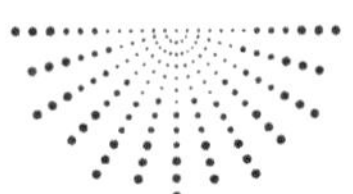

What is going to keep us on track?

Practicing self-compassion

Be nice to yourself! You are the person you spend the most time with and I can guarantee you that you're pretty darn great. If that mean inner critic dares to speak up, I want you to tell it to do one! Now I know I've said it thousands of times before, but you must must must show yourself the same kindness that you show to others *(and I promise I'll do the same.)*

Listening to our bodies

We have to practice this more and more. If you're tired, rest. If you feel like alone time, schedule it in. If you feel like socialising, schedule that in too. A key feature of recovery is repairing our relationship with our body, listening to its needs and not mistreating it anymore. That means setting boundaries with our energy and time. It's not selfish. It's essential in our modern world.

Using our go-to coping skills

I'm sure by now you've built up a bunch of really great coping skills, habits, practices *(call them what you will)* which are super supportive. However, if you find any old habits wanting to creep on in, take to the pages and write it out. Reassess what's working for you and what isn't. Sometimes listing out all the options we have in times of need can be a great reminder of just how many things we have up our sleeve!

Communicating any wobbles with others

There are going to be times when old habits or thoughts might come knocking on the door. If you feel anything like that trying to creep on in, let someone you trust know. You can reassure them that you're not planning on engaging with any old habits, but you'd like to talk out what's been going on in your head. Having these thoughts and talking about this stuff doesn't mean you've relapsed, it's all part of recovery.

Protecting yourself from diet culture

Don't get sucked into the BS. Remember, every diet culture scream is just a bid to make you feel bad about yourself so people can profit off it. They want us to reject our bodies so that they can sell us something to 'fix' them. Continue to be selective of who you listen to. Continue to be selective of what media you consume. And know that you are enough, as you are right now and always will be.

JOURNALING FAQS

I feel blocked, like I can't write anything, how do I get past this?

I assure you the words are in there just waiting to come out, but sometimes they need a little coaxing. When it comes to journaling, sometimes we can feel a real 'block'. This can be for a myriad of reasons, and I invite you to first get curious with why that might be happening for you.

Ask yourself: *What is the feeling that sits behind being 'blocked'? Am I attaching something to the outcome? What is it about it that feels difficult? Can I pinpoint it?*

Whatever it is for you, I find closing my eyes and taking some deep breaths in and out prior to writing can help. During this moment of calm, place your hand on your heart and repeat the words: *I am free to be me.*

I want you to know that this is *your* space where anything goes. This practice and your words are for you and you only. Journaling is not about getting it 'right' or crafting a 'perfect' piece of writing. It's simply a different way of communicating with yourself, an outlet, a space to let it all out and you deserve that. Approach it with freedom in your heart.

I feel scared, too scared to write anything, how do I get past this?

This is one I hear a lot and that's typically because when we're living with an ed, we disconnect from how we are truly feeling. When we are then faced with reconnecting with what's going on inside of us, that can feel really scary. Please know you are not alone in this whatsoever.

Similar to dealing with a 'block' I find closing your eyes and taking some deep breaths in and out prior to writing can help. During this moment of calm, place your hand on your heart and repeat the words: *It's okay to feel. I'm allowed to feel. My feelings are valid here. They are welcome.*

Now if you've tried a prompt and are sat shaking your head, thinking *'I don't know, I can't do this'*, my advice is always to simplify your practice. If the prompts are too much, bring it back to the five daily questions. Continue with those until you have got into the habit of reconnecting with how you are feeling. If even the *Daily* questions feel too much in this moment, know that you can come back to it tomorrow and try again.

I'm worried about messing up the pages of my notebook, what should I do?

I would start out by reminding yourself of your journals purpose. This is a tool to support you on your healing journey. It's not meant to be pristine or scribble free. It can help to zoom out here and imagine if you were to look back on it ten years from now. Would you be cranky about a misspelled word, or would you be proud of the incredible progress you made? I can almost guarantee you it would be the latter.

Now in terms of practical advice, some people find having two journals can help to eliminate this concern. One is the rough unfiltered draft, and one is a 'final' draft that they frequently refer back to. Some people copy out their *why* and affirmations into a smaller notebook. Some people scribble all over the first page of their notebook to get comfortable and some people write out quotes about mistakes and acceptance to help inspire them. I invite you to experiment here and find what works for you.

I don't like writing with a pen and paper, I prefer typing, can I do the journal prompts that way?

Of course! You can do the prompts in whatever way works best for you.

Though, in my personal experience I've found the truth to flow out of me more freely when I put pen to paper. It just doesn't feel the same typing on my phone or on my laptop, so that's always my preference.

However, if you are feeling resistance to working with a pen and paper, try it for a week and if it's still a no go, stick to digital. I'm not a fan of dictating the 'right' way to do things, the main thing here is that you choose the method that works best for you. This is *your* recovery.

I don't feel like a particular journal prompt applies to me, should I still do it?

Oftentimes I've thought this when doing other people's prompts, but then I've found after thinking on it for a few minutes something actually comes to me.

My advice would be to sit with the prompt for a few minutes, re-read it a few times, then close your eyes and see if anything comes to mind.

If it still doesn't, it might be that it's not something you've experienced. If so, you can either move on or just jot down your thoughts around the subject.

I designed the prompts because oftentimes I didn't know what to write about in my own recovery or what I even needed to address to heal, but they're based on my experience and therefore they might not always resonate with you, but I hope they mostly do.

I'm finding it hard to make it a regular habit, how can I overcome this?

The best way to form a new habit and make it a go-to in your day is to get clear on what it is and how it's going to look.

Now, what I mean by that is, setting yourself a particular time of day to journal at, selecting a particular length of time that you will journal for and also selecting the location of where you're going to do it.

For example:

I will journal for 10 mins upon waking in my bed.

Length of time = 10 mins

Time of day = Morning, upon waking

Location = In bed

I will journal for 15 mins as soon as I get home from work and have changed into my comfy clothes, on the couch.

Length of time = 15 mins

Time of day = Evening, after work

Location = Couch

I'm finding it overwhelming and hard to get started, any suggestions?

If it's the prompts in particular that you are finding challenging, my advice is always the same, simplify your practice. *Remember the five daily questions?* Just focus on them.

Your journaling practice has to work for you, the intention is to have it support you and if that means keeping it simple. Then please do that. And remember, there is no right and wrong. This is *your* recovery.

BOOKS I MENTIONED

Stage Two: Headspace

Robbins, M. (2021). *The High 5 Habit: Take Control of Your Life with One Simple Habit*. United States: Hay House.

Stage Three: Reflections

Sturino, K. (2021). *Body Talk: How to Embrace Your Body and Start Living Your Best Life.* New York: Clarkson Potter.

ACKNOWLEDGMENTS

My eternal thanks goes to my loving husband for his support in all that I do.

My extended gratitude goes to all my clients and workshop participants who have shared their lives and recovery journey with me.

Putting pen to paper continues to change my life for the better and I hope it can do the same for you too.

ABOUT THE AUTHOR

Sophie B is passionate about empowering individuals to take charge of their recovery journeys. Having walked the path herself, she developed the transformative Recover You Journaling Method during her own recovery. This approach combines a multi-staged self-reflective practice, daily strategies and practical steps for anyone striving to overcome an eating disorder.

Through writing, speaking, and leading workshops, Sophie shares her story and insights to inspire others to reclaim their lives. Her mission is to remind those in recovery that healing is possible - and to encourage them to take one meaningful step towards it today.

Connect with Sophie on social media: @letsrecoveryou.

Made in the USA
Las Vegas, NV
02 January 2025

15687744R00089